A SOTA Publishing Book

© SOTA Publishing
All rights reserved

ISBN 0-9765115-0-9 Paperback

Printed in the United States of America 2005

25 LESSONS IN OFFICIAL

JIU JITSU

AS TAUGHT IN THE
JAPANESE ARMY & NAVY

INCLUDING THE VITAL TOUCH,
METHODS OF VIVIFICATION, AND
ADVANCED COMBAT TRICKS

BY
DR. G. KIKUTA
-1905

NOW INCLUDES ADDITIONAL COMMENTARY
BY WORLD RENOWNED PRESSURE POINT
SPECIALIST, MARK KLINE
-2005

INTRODUCTION

Jiu-Jitsu is a system of self-defense and of physical and moral training. It aims to overcome brute strength with skill and science; it compensates for superior strength and muscular development. It is highly scientific, exemplifying mechanical, psychological and anatomical laws. In Japan it is taught in its milder form in all the schools and colleges, and in its more advanced form in the military and naval academies. Every soldier of the Mikado is skilled in the art. It is to the persistent practice of Jiu-Jitsu that the Japanese attribute their courage and success in battle, their wonderful powers of physical endurance, and their coolness and self-reliance in the face of sudden danger.

In these twenty-five lessons are taught the advanced methods of self-defense, the "vital-touches" and methods of "vivification" and the secret combat tricks by which the ancient Samurai defended themselves unarmed, against an assailant.

Students of Jiu-Jitsu are cautioned against using these "vital-touches" except in the most extreme cases and then only in defense of life or honor.

Dr. G. Kikuda (1905)

I came across this book many years ago. I had always thought it an important historical work, which documented the field of research (Kyusho Jitsu – Pressure Point Fighting) that I have been involved in for most of my martial arts career. Each lesson is represented completely and intact including the original photos that have been cleaned up. At the end of each lesson, I have used my expertise in the art of Kyusho Jitsu to add to the original manuscript. Also included at the end of each lesson, are ways to increase the efficiency of each technique. It is my hope that this information be preserved and be used as a link to the past. It was also my intention to expand on the wealth of knowledge of the original author.

Mark Kline (2005)

ii

TABLE OF CONTENTS

DEEP BREATHING

The Japanese are believers in Nature's cure. They believe that an artificial remedy can never be superior to Nature's and so they seek a natural cure for every ill. A druggist in Japan would be left to eke out a bare existence, and a doctor would be patronized only by the aged and infirmed.

The Japanese believe that plenty of fresh air is more conducive to good health than anything else. Their dwelling houses are better ventilated than any European structures. They are built mostly with only two parallel walls. The ends are left open, and during the daytime the air is allowed to circulate freely through the house. In the summer time the open ends are usually hung with bamboo screens, and in the winter a sliding screen door, or shoji, is used on the open ends to prevent the direct draught. These shoji are rain and wind proof, but are in a sense porous and admit a free circulation of air. They are made of thin, but strong Japanese paper, which, in Japan, takes the place of window glass.

The Japanese are not afraid of a draught. Even in their sleeping apartments they allow the cold night air to circulate freely. If the night were unusually cold, they add more covering, but they never close their windows. This practice, if followed by Western people, might prove disastrous to them, as, owing to Western customs and manners of life, they are more subject to colds and more sensitive to draughts than the Japanese. But certainly Western people would be healthier if their sleeping apartments were better ventilated.

In the summer time no harm can result from throwing the windows of the sleeping apartment wide open, and allowing the air to circulate freely. In the winter time a screen of very fine, woven wire may be placed in the window in the same manner as fly screens are placed in the summer. This fine wire screen will allow a free circulation of air, and will prevent a draught. These screens an be made at a very small expense and are really better than any patent ventilator which is on the market.

In Japan consumption is a disease, which is almost unknown, and this condition is attributed to the style of dwelling houses, which permit one to life as Nature requires, i.e. with an abundant supply of fresh air.

It is a custom among Japanese business and professional men, and others who do not belong to the laboring classes, to take a morning stroll, just before sunrise. These morning walks are taken either in the gardens, parks, or along the country roads; and the custom is not neglected even in the coldest winter days. This strolling exercise is thoroughly enjoyed by every man whose calling does not require him to begin his day's labor at a very early hour.

The day is never so beautiful as it is just at sunrise, which in the Japanese Islands is a sight not soon forgotten, especially during the Spring and Autumn, when a light mist, which is formed by the condensation of atmospheric vapor, hangs over the land.

Deep draughts of fresh air are inhaled and exhaled, and the stroller returns to his home refreshed and invigorated and amply repaid for his fifteen-minute walk.

Americans who have never indulged in this custom will experience a most pleasant sensation after the first morning stroll and will need no other inventive to induce them to continue the exercise.

To those who find it inconvenient to exercise their lungs in this manner, the subjoined exercises will be beneficial if followed in-doors. But care must be taken to have the room well ventilated. Any room except the sleeping apartment will be best for these exercises.

EXERCISE NO. 1

Go to the open window in a room that is well ventilated. Stand erect and force the air out of the lungs by folding the arms (A) across the chest and

drawing the upper arms close to the side. Then allow the arms to relax and hang at the sides (B) and inhale deeply trough the nostrils, drinking as much of the fresh air as the lungs will contain. In inhaling, breathe first from the abdomen and then distend the chest. Hold the breath for fifteen seconds, and exhale slowly through the mouth.

On first practicing this exercise, a person who is not accustomed to deep breathing will experience a slight dizziness, which will wear off after a few days'

A

practice. (This exercise should be practiced five times every morning, immediately upon rising.)

B

2

EXERCISE NO. II

Stand erect with the heels together and arms hanging loosely at the sides. Inhale deeply through the nostrils, taking as much air into the lungs as possible. Then slowly raise the arms over the head (C), and clasp and interlace

C   D   E

the fingers, turning the palms of the hands outward. Then bend the body at the waist as far as possible, to the right (D) and to the left (E). Then exhale slowly. (This exercise should be practiced five times each morning.)

EXERCISE NO. III

Inhale deeply, filing the lungs to their fullest capacity, then raise the arms and interlace the fingers, placing the palms of the hands at the back of the head (F). Then rise up on the toes (G), making the body perfectly rigid, and while in this condition walk across the room without touching the heels to the floor. Then exhale slowly and repeat the exercise. (This is a splendid exercise for strengthening the lungs and developing the chest, and it may be practiced both morning and evening as many times as one can do so without tiring oneself.)

F

G

Each exercise will be further explained below. I wanted to preserve the original manuscript as it originally looked. As there were no pictures for the breathing exercises, I placed them above for visual purposes.

EXERCISE NO. I

When you fold the arms across the chest in the manner shown in Illustration A, you are stimulating the Lung 1 & 2 points (Illustration H). The explanation of the points names, etc. are spoken about in Lesson No 25.

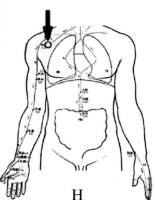

A point known as Heart 8 ("Lesser Yin Mansion"), located on the inside of the palm between the pinky and ring finger (between the 4th and 5th metacarpal), will automatically lay over these points. "Connecting the dots" stimulates these points to assist in "opening up" the lung meridian. Heart 8 is the fire point on the heart meridian.

According to Traditional Chinese Medicine, stimulating the lungs in this manner will allow the lungs to operate more efficiently. Most people are shallow breathers and when at rest, rarely use more than 20% of their lung capicity. As spoken about above, their may be a slight dizziness when the exercise is started. This is due to toxins in the lungs being released and thus the lungs "cleared".

Our body operates on a more optimal level when the "parts" are taken care of. Proper breathing is vital when it comes to good health and all martial arts include some type of breathing techniques as a part of their system.

H

EXERCISE NO. II

Most people will not take the time to take care of themselves properly. This is a normal thing in today's world and was not much different at the turn of the previous century. Exercise No. II is a small piece of an exercise that I practice called the Ba Duan Gin.

As instructed above, you are to clasp your hands together and raise them

4

over your head with the palms up. This stretches the meridians of the arms

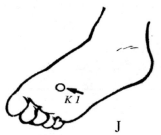

(Illustration I). Bending to the side, stretches and stimulates the meridians of the torso. Stimulating the meridians in this manner keeps them "tuned up."

For more information on the Ba Duan Gin, please log onto Kyusho.com and click on the link for Chinese Yoga.

I

EXERCISE NO. III

This exercise instructs you to stand on the balls of your feet. There is a point called Kidney 1 ("Bubbling Spring") located between the big toe and the second toe on the ball of the foot (Illustration J). Energy enters the body from the ground at Kidney 1, rises up the front of the body and exits through the Bladder Meridian in the heel. Standing on your toes is designed to "take in" energy and "store it."

K 1

J

Interlacing your fingers and placing your palms on the back of your head is designed to "keep" the energy in the upper half of the body. There is a point called Governor Vessel 16 ("Wind Palace"), located directly above the hairline in the depression between the trapezius muscles of both sides (Illustration K). This point is known to calm the mind. Heart 8 on both hands will sit in close proximity to this point, thus "stimulating" it.

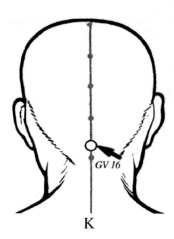

GV 16

K

LESSON ONE

TAKA-BASAMI—"TAKING-HOLD-UP-HIGH"

The following methods can be employed very effectively in defense against attack by an assailant who may attempt to spar. We will assume that the assailant has made a left-arm thrust. Illustration No. 1 shows the defendant in the act of parrying the thrust by forcing the assailant's arm obliquely upward with his right hand. At the same time stepping forward behind assailant's advanced foot, the defendant then quickly passes his left arm underneath the raised arm of the assailant and around his neck and brings the right hand to the center of the assailant's back.

IL. 1

IL. 2

Care must be taken not to strike the assailant's back with force. The right hand should merely be pressed against his back. A severe blow or too strong a pressure would render the assailant momentarily helpless and might result in serious injury to him.

Illustration No. 2 shows the position assumed by the assailant and defendant. It will be noted that the assailant's left arm is helpless and that he is unable to reach the defendant with his right arm, owing to the fact that his body is held firmly in position by the defendant's left arm, which passes tightly around his neck, almost shutting off his breath. Should he try to turn his body so as to bring his right arm into effect, he would suffer intense pain, owing to the pressure of the defendant's right hand at the small of his back.

These two steps illustrate the most important as well as the most difficult part of the defense, for if these be correctly effected the defense is practically ended, as the assailant is now at the mercy of the defendant.

The success in obtaining results depends more upon the defendant's knowledge of the assailants method, than skill in Jiu-Jitsu; but whenever an assailant assumes the position of attack with the left arm thrust forward, the defendant can invariably apply this method most effectively.

In using Illustrations Nos. 1 and 2, to show the method of procedure by the defendant, it is assumed that the assailant, places himself in a position which lays him open to this method of counter-attack. The same

6

means may be employed should the assailant thrust forward his right arm instead of the left, in which case the defendant must assume a position directly opposite to that shown in Illustration No.1. It is better, however, that the defendant wait for his opportunity to make a counter-attack in the manner illustrated. He will usually find this method the most effective.

Before proceeding to place the assailant in a state of final "submission," a few words may be said in regard to the advantage the defendant has thus far attained. The familiar mechanical principle of the lever is here suggested. The defendant still keeping his right hand pressed firmly against the assailant's back, steps still further behind him and thrusts his left hip quickly behind the assailant.

The defendant may now, with comparatively little effort, lift the assailant's feet from the ground by stooping forward: at the same time the defendant should throw his right hand behind him and grasp the assailant's leg. The body of the assailant is then raised with very little effort to the position shown in Illustration No. 3.

IL. 3

Two methods of forcing the final "submission" of the assailant are now available. One, is to throw him violently to the ground by releasing the grasp of his leg, retaining the grasp on his neck and giving a quick twist to the shoulder. This method is not advisable, as the fall might disable or injure him.

The second method is to lay him gently on his back and effect a "submission" by the method hereinafter mentioned. If the assailant be a heavy man, it is advisable that the defendant should not attempt to throw him forcibly, as such a method might mean injury to both; however, if the assailant is experienced in Jiu-Jitsu, he ought to know how to land after the fall, so that he would be unhurt and could then quickly recover and renew the attack.

Assuming that the defendant has chosen the second method of disposing of his assailant, he will now proceed to affect a final "submission." In laying the assailant on the ground, the defendant tightens his grasp on the assailant's neck and at the same time releases his grasp of the assailant' leg, swinging the assailant's body to the floor in front of him.

While in the position shown in Illustration No. 3, the assailant's body is somewhat strained, that is, it is bent by the force applied at two points, the neck and the leg; hence, when the hold of the leg is released suddenly and at the same instant the grasp of the neck is tightened, the body tends to spring.

It is by this utilization of the force of inertia, that the body of the assailant is quickly brought to the front and laid down with very little exertion. Then and only then does the defendant release his grasp of the neck, but it is not withdrawn entirely, for the hand of this arm is now at the neck and chin of his assailant, as shown in Illustration No. 4, and his knee holds the assailant's body to the floor, at the same time rendering helpless his left arm by bending it backward over the thigh.

This position illustrates one of the Jiu-Jitsu methods of enforcing "submission." A "submission" is always final and decisive. It means an advantage, which when once gained, places the opponent in such a position that he is utterly unable to renew the attack until released. In short, it is a state of complete control of the adversary and any attempt to recover from it is vain.

IL. 4

The "submission" shown in Illustration No. 4, is effected at three points, viz., the chin, the side and the arm; of these three, the first and second are "death points" and the latter, dislocation of the arm. The assailant is thus held down until he yields, that is, until he confesses his willingness to do so by word or sign; usually the latter, which in a formal contest is made by striking the ground with the free arm or the foot.

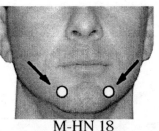

M-HN 18

We are going to focus on the "submission" of this technique. Dr. Kikuta has mentioned 3 points that, through diagram and discussion, I will elaborate on. The chin point that he refers to is an extraordinary point known as M-HN 18 (M-HN = Major Head & Neck). This points also sits on top of the mental foramen. The mental nerve runs through a hole in the mandible. When pressed down and in (see arrows) towards the opposite shoulder, it releases the sternocleidomastoid muscle, thus enabling you to turn the head of the opponent. When this point is lightly struck in the same direction, it can cause dizziness, when struck with force, it can cause unconsciousness. Death may not necessarily occur from the blow, but the opponent will not have the ability to break his fall, thus adding to the danger of this point.

In the next part of the technique, you are to kneel on the opponent's side on a point known as Liver 13. Known as "Chapter Gate, Liver 13 is the warning point for the Spleen. Points that have the word "gate" in its name are of particular importance to martial artists. These are excellent points with which to "enter" the nervous system of your opponent.

In this particular technique you are kneeling on your opponent to keep him from rising. His attempts to resist cause him much pain, thus aiding in the "submission."

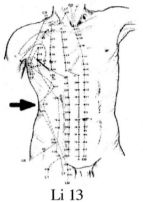

Front view of Torso

Li 13

The Triple Warmer meridian, also goes by the name of San Jiao (three burners). The author has stated that this point is useful in dislocation of the arm. Triple Warmer 11 is also known as "Cooling Gulf," which is used to treat motor impairment and paint in the shoulder and arm.

TW 11

It is a point that needs a rubbing action (see arrow) to release the joint. The elbow is best dislocated this way. It is one of the strongest joints in the body and not easily broken by a strike.

For purposes of the technique described above and in subsequent lessons, this point has been exclusively used to dislocate the arm through a prying (rubbing) action. For optimum effectiveness, TW 11 needs rubbing in the direction that the nerve runs, which in this case is from the top of the arm down. Rubbing in a perpendicular action will not have the same effectiveness as a parallel rubbing action.

9

LESSON TWO

KEAGE—"KICKING-UP"

Generally speaking Jiu-Jitsu aims only at final "submission" with little regard to the means employed in attaining this result. But in some instances a contest may be terminated without "submission." For example, the defendant may be thrown forcibly to the ground with the result that he is injured to such an extent as to render further resistance impossible.

Keage or "kicking-up" is a means of attack, which aims at this result. The assailant falls down before the defendant in such a manner as to utilize the momentum generated by his exertion, and tries to force him over on his back. The principle of Jiu-Jitsu, that the strength of the defendant should be utilized as much as possible in bringing about his defeat, is here well illustrated.

In this attack, the assailant grasps, either the coat lapels or the shoulders of the defendant with both hands as shown in Illustration No. 5. This will force the defendant to defend himself by grasping the assailant's shoulder. The assailant then sways the defendant backwards and forward, inviting resistance and a similar effort from him.

IL. 5

The moment the defendant retaliates, the assailant feigns to fall backward, and in falling raises his right leg quickly and places his foot on the defendant's lower abdomen, as shown in Illustration No. 6. The assailant then falls to the floor as shown in Illustration No. 7, kicking upward with considerable force the body of the defendant, which is flying over him.

The momentum generated by the assailant's fall carries the defendant over him with great force. When the defendant is directly over the assailant, the latter releases the hold on his coat lapels in such a manner as to aid in giving his body momentum. The result is that the defendant is thrown some distance.

The question might here be raised as to the probable result to the defendant of such a fall. At first it would seem that the force of the throw could in a manner be eased if the defendant would not lessen his grasp on the assailant's shoulders. It would appear that such an action would check the momentum of the defendant's body in such a manner as to dislocate the bones of the neck, or to cause concussion of the brain. The assailant would, in such a case, be perfectly safe, since the body of the defendant,

10

IL. 6

by the force, which had been generated, must land completely over and clear of the assailant. On the other hand it is possible for the defendant to permit the headlong fall by holding tightly to the assailant's shoulders until the defendant's body strikes the floor, thus escaping the fatality mentioned.

But this is a very difficult thing to do , and it is far less dangerous for the defendant, if he does not attempt to resist the throw, but allows himself to continue his onward course. By a quick turn of his body, when clear of the assailant, he will land on his feet and hands.

An expert Jiu-Jitsuian, when he finds himself at the mercy of his assailant, promptly prepares for the inevitable and allows himself to be tossed over the assailant's body. He can even direct the force of the assailant's throw in such a manner as to control his body while in the air so as to land on his feet or hands.

IL. 7

One experienced in the Jiu-Jitsu system ought to be able to protect himself from injury if thrown in this manner on a stone pavement. The danger of the fall can be avoided if the defendant aids rather than retards the assailant by giving a spring just before being tossed up and over, thus adding force to the momentum of his body. If this is practiced repeatedly the defendant can, with training easily land on his feet.

As will be seen, this method of attack does not always result in victory for the assailant, for it often happens that one skilled in Jiu-Jitsu purposely invites such an attack, and then while in the act of being thrown over his assailant's body, inflicts a severe if not fatal blow, and after landing safely turns quickly and renews the attack before the assailant has a chance to regain his feet.

On brief, the chief aim of the assailant in this method of attack is to disable his enemy temporarily or permanently. The fact that a final "submission" cannot be attained by this method makes it advisable that beginners should apply its principles with utmost care, being careful not to injure the defendant. The throw should be made only under the most favorable conditions.

In a contest between Japanese wrestlers this mode of attack is considered one of the most effective. It is also a splendid means of defense, but it requires alertness and frequent practice to insure unfailing results.

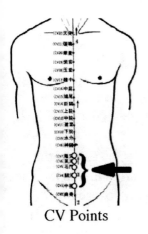

CV Points

The Conception Vessel, or centerline, runs up the center of the front of the body much like the spine runs along the center of the back. The act of "Kicking Up," as the author reports, "should be made only under the most favorable of conditions." When you kick or put pressure with your foot into Conception Vessel points below the navel (CV 3 - CV 7), the hips of the opponent go back as the upper body bends forward. Breaking your opponent's balance by using these points, you are making the conditions more, "favorable."

CV 3 - "Middle Extremity"
Located along the midline approximately 4 inches below the navel.

CV 4 - "Gate to the original Qi"
Located along the midline approximately 3 inches below the navel.

CV 5 - "Stone Door"
Located along the midline approximately 2 inches below the navel.

CV 6 - "Sea of Qi"
Located along the midline approximately 1.5 inches below the navel.

CV 7 - "Yin Crossing"
Located along the midline approximately 1 inche below the navel.

* For more information about point names, their meaning, and more, please refer to the bibliography section for a listing of references.

LESSON THREE

MAKIKOMI—"WINDING-UP."

The required opportunity for beginning this method of attack may be presented either at the beginning or during a contest. It is , however, more apt to be presented at the initiative step or at the beginning of a renewal of attack. The signal for attack is when the defendant first lays hold of the coat lapel of the assailant. (Illustration No. 8 Defendant on the left and assailant on the right.)

As soon as the coat lapel is seized the assailant grasps the arm of the defendant at the wrist with his left hand and steps forward with his left foot (assuming the position shown in Illustration No. 9), with his back toward the defendant. The left arm of the defendant is thus "wound-up" and rendered helpless.

IL. 8

IL. 9

The first step of the offense has now been taken. It would appear that at this moment the assailant is exposing himself to his enemy, who, it seems, is in a position to strike him in the back with his free right arm. The danger, however, is only momentary. The action of the assailant in "winding-up" the left arm of the defendant is so quick and decisive that the possibilities of a counter-attack are not so apparent in an actual contest. Moreover it will be seen later on (in the discussion of Makikomi-Defensive) that the opening here shown is not used for the defense against this attack.

The next step of the assailant is to throw his hips against the defendant's side and then to stoop forward until his knees and his free hand touch the floor (Illustration No. 10.) It will be noticed that the hold upon the wrist of the defendant has not been altered since the first step. The position thus far effected is preparatory to a throw.

The entrapped arm of the defendant is now drawn further in underneath the body of the assailant so as to throw the weight of the defendant's body on the back of the assailant. Then the assailant by a quick swing of his body to the left throws the defendant completely over him, the defendant landing at the assailant's back. The assailant still keeping his grasp on the defendant's wrist, simply reclines over the body of the defendant (Illustration No 11.)

13

IL. 10

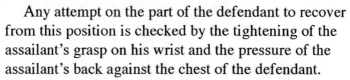

Any attempt on the part of the defendant to recover from this position is checked by the tightening of the assailant's grasp on his wrist and the pressure of the assailant's back against the chest of the defendant.

The "submission," in this case is effected by twisting or bending the entrapped arm of the defendant. The bending is accomplished by pressing the upper arm of the defendant between the chest and arm of the assailant, and then bending back the forearm of the defendant. The pain thus produced would alone be sufficient to exact a "submission" from the defendant. Care must be taken not to twist the arm of the defendant while it is thus bent backward at the elbow as it would result in dislocation.

IL. 11

Success in this attack depends on the alertness of the assailant. In the series of illustrations here shown, it would seem that the assailant lays himself open to counter-attack on two different occasions, but so swift are his movements that in reality the defendant has little opportunity to resist. After his arm is once grasped and "wound-up" he has absolutely no chance of recovery, unless he be skilled in the art of Jiu-Jitsu.

TW 11

As has been stated in previous lessons, Triple Warmer 11, is the "rub" point used to create "submission." The best way for this point to be of use, is to turn your opponent's hand palm up (IL. 11). Applying pressure on the wrist (the lever) in a downward manner, you simultaneously apply pressure upwards against the arm with your torso (the fulcrum). Though it would take a quick jerk of the arm to possibly dislocate it, you would definately hyperextend the arm, rendering it temporarily useless. This is a great point for submission.

14

LESSON FOUR

UDE-MAKIKOMI—"ARM TWISTING."

In this operation, the hold on the scarf (coat lapel) is the opening signal for this attack. The assailant grasps the wrist of the defendant's extended left arm in the his left hand, then thrusts his right arm underneath the extended left arm of the defendant and grasps the defendant's right scarf.

The assailant then swings the defendant's body to his side as in Illustration No. 12 (assailant at the right and defendant at the left in illustration.) This position gives the assailant the advantage, inasmuch as his right arm is thrust under the left arm of the defendant and can be used as a fulcrum upon which the defendant's arm may be bent.

When this position is assumed the assailant quickly thrusts his head underneath the crossed arms (Illustration No. 13), turning completely around with his back toward defendant's left side. The assailant then falls on his back to the floor (Illustration No. 14.) The defendant by this process of "arm-twisting" ought to be thrown on his back, his body turning a complete somersault (Illustration No. 14, defendant's body in the act of turning.)

IL. 12

At this moment the defendant has had to release his hold of the assailant's wrists, in order to use his freed arm in supporting his body so as to avert the impending headlong fall.

This process may be more easily understood by imagining a wheel being turned by a handle attached at right angles to the rim of the wheel, the operator of the wheel turning his body completely around with each revolution of the wheel instead of letting the handle slip through his hand as is usually done.

In this exercise, the body of the defendant is the wheel, the arm the handle and the assailant the operator.

By carefully following Illustrations Nos. 12, 13, and 14, it will be noted that the assailant's body has made one more turn in the process than the defendant's. It must therefore follow that if the assailant has retained his grasp of the defendant's scarf and left wrist during the entire operation, the defendant must come to the floor on his back in a position almost at right angles to the body of the assailant.

IL. 13

15

IL. 14

The final "submission" in this operation is attained through the "arm-breaking" process.

The assailant having forced the defendant to the floor, pushes his right arm underneath the entrapped right arm of the defendant, and using this as a fulcrum, bends the defendant's entrapped arm backward at the elbow. At the same time he twists the wrist in such a manner as to cause defendant "excruciating pain."

This action on the part of the assailant is done so quickly that the defendant does not have time to recover from his fall before his arm is bent and his wrist twisted. He is, therefore, wholly unable to recover himself and is forced to "submission."

Referring again to Illustration No. 12, the assailant should step away from the defendant as far as possible, in order to keep his body clear of the defendant while pushing his head underneath the crossed arms. 'this is, perhaps, the most difficult step in the exercise.

If properly effected, and the grasp of defendant's wrists maintained, his body must come to the floor, as any resistance on his part would result in a broken arm.

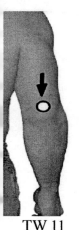

TW 11

This technique use the same Triple Warmer 11 point in a different manner. Previously, the point was used for submission. Now this point is used to throw your opponent.

This point is easily accessible. There is a simple way to access this point, as long as you follow certain principles. If you take an arrow from the back of the arm, through, to the front, perpendicular to the arm, this arrow will give you the direction that you need to apply pressure for best results. At the same time the direction that the point needs to be rubbed is down towards the hand. This two way pressure causes the muscles supporting the elbow joint to relax(Cross Extensor Reflex Action), thus enabling you to throw your opponent and/or injure his arm.

LESSON FIVE

OENAGE—"TOSSING OVERHEAD"

The fact that Jiu-Jitsu, the art of weaponless warfare, was primarily intended as a means of self defense must be kept in mind.

This lesson, while considered offensive is really a lesson in defense. The one who is the defendant all along, is in reality the one who makes the attack but the terms assailant and defendant will be used as in all the former lessons.

The assailant allows the defendant to grapple with him from behind, permitting him to throw his arms around the assailant's chest, pinning his arms (Illustration No. 15.)

To loosen the hold of the defendant is the first move of the assailant. This is, of course, not an easy affair, if the defendant who has the advantage is the stronger, but where the strength is about equal, the loosening ought to be done on the part of the assailant, by simply raising his arms in a forcible manner (Illustration No. 16).

This, however, involves only ordinary strength. The loosening of the hold is accomplished most readily by the assailant bending his knees at the moment he raises and extends his arms. The left hand of the assailant should hold the right hand of the defendant. This hold should be continued while the assailant is kneeling, and, as soon as he begins to recover his freedom, he reaches up and seizes the defendant by the shoulder (Illustration No. 17.)

IL. 15

It will be noticed that the assailant rests on his left knee while his right knee bends but does not touch the floor and that the tip of the right foot of the assailant is resting on the right foot of the defendant.

IL. 16

IL. 17

This is the "tossing" attitude, the "toss" being to the right of the assailant. The defendant is here hindered from shifting his right foot for the purpose of preventing the throw, because of the pressure exerted by assailant's toes upon his foot.

The "toss" is accomplished by the assailant pulling down on the

17

defendant's right shoulder which turns him on his side and throws him upon the floor on his back, thus breaking the grasp shown in Illustration No. 17, which allows the defendant to be tossed free from the assailant except that the assailant continues the same grasp upon the defendant's right hand until the last.

As the defendant falls upon the floor, the right knee of the assailant is immediately bent over his side which prevents him from rising from his position while the assailant prepares for the act of "submission."

The "submission" is mainly an "arm-breaking" process. The right arm of the defendant is bent back against the assailant's right knee which also aids in bending the arm.

Beside breaking the arm in the "submission" two other points are touched, namely the side and the chin. The last two are fatal points. It was noted in a previous lesson that a delicate spot to deal the death-blow could easily be located on the side. Care in holding the defendant as indicated insures "submission."

Front view of Torso

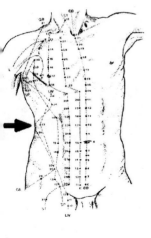

The submission that the author is referring to is the same one used in previous lessons. Liver 13 is an excellent way to follow up on a throw due to the sensative nature of this point.

The arm bar uses the same Triple Warmer 11 point that is used for "submission" throughout this system.

An important side note: When points are used in combinations that that adhere to the laws of acupuncture, they become more potent. Due to the internal dynamics of the body, some points are more powerful than others (*Mu & Shu Points).

Warning points on the front and back of the body that are directly associated with the organs or bowels.)

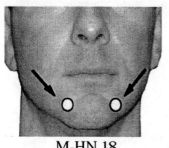

M-HN 18

The mental foramen point (M-HN 18), as decribed earlier, is an extremely potent point to use in self defense. The pain that one feels from a "touch" at this point is similar to one as if you had gone to the dentist. Done properly, your opponent quickly loses his will to continue struggling as each time he renews his attack, he hurts himself. It is quite possible for him to inflict severe pain on himself if he does decide to struggle. You will find that when you utilize this point properly, it will be easy to subdue a larger, stronger opponent.

Stomach 5 is a point found midway between the chin and the corner of the jaw, is an additional point that has been added to this text. "Big Welcome," as the point is known in chinese, sits on the 7th cranial nerve (facial nerve). The angle and direction to hit this point is in towards the opposite side of the head and back towards the ear. This backwards motion traces the facial nerve and your opponent will experience, with a light touch, a slight buzzing accompanied with

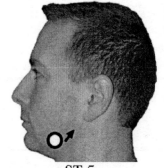

ST 5

the sensation of someone running their fingers through your hair on the side hit. Be careful with using extreme force as this can cause unconsciousness and your opponent can be further injured as he hits the floor without being able to control his fall.

LESSON SIX

KOSHI-GARUMA — "HAUNCH WHEEL."

In the operation of Koshi-Garuma a simple means of effecting an opening is afforded by the defendant when he selects for his grapple a hold with his left hand (Illustration No. 18) on the assailant's scarf.

The assailant with his left hand then seizes the attacking arm of the defendant at the wrist (Illustration No. 18,) and, striding quickly forward with his left foot begins to "wind- in" the defendant's entrapped arm under his own arm and around his side (Illustration No. 19.)

This stride should be taken so as to avoid bringing the feet of the assailant and defendant too close together as the assailant will need room for his next move.

With his left side against the left side of the defendant, the assailant continues the "winding-in" process until he stands in the position shown in Illustration No. 20. This attitude is the result of a long stride which he makes behind the defendant and by means of which he almost has the feet of the defendant between his own (Illustration No. 20.)

IL.18

The assailant's feet should be placed as far apart as is consistent with a secure footing for he will need this in order to be successful in the next step of the operation.

It will be observed that there is an analogy thus far between Koshi-Guruma, and Makikomi. This similarity, however, is confined to the initiatory grapples of the contestants and by the side-by-side position assumed for the purpose of lifting (Illustrations No. 18 and No. 19.)

In Koshi-garuma, the assailant stands behind the defendant when he lifts the defendant; but in Makikomi he stands in front of the defendant.

The substitution of a method employed in Makikomi might here be made for the corresponding one of Koshi-Garuma. The choice depends upon circumstances attending the grapples and the making of the footings.

If the assailant finds that he can bewilder the defendant by swerving from one method to another, he should do so, as one of the cardinal principles of Jiu-Jitsu is to employ strategy wherever and whenever is

IL.19

20

can successfully be done.

A favorable moment at which to substitute Makikomi or Ogoshi for Koshi-Garuma is when the assailant stands beside the defendant as in Illustration No. 19. If the assailant finds that his footing has fallen short of what he has intended for the operation of Koshi-Garuma, he should step in front of the defendant and finish the operation according to Makikomi or Ogoshi.

So, too, in Makikomi or Ogoshi if the contestant should miss his required footing by taking too long a stride, he may resort to the methods of Koshi-Garuma for defense.

When the assailant has assumed the position shown in Illustration No. 20, he has a firm hold on the defendant's right thigh with his right hand, supplemented by the position of his arm. He now stoops, drawing down

IL.20

the "wound-in" arm of the defendant, which is firmly held under his own arm and around his side and back (Illustration No. 20.) With a quick lift of the shoulders, the assailant raises the body of the defendant clear of the floor and swings him over his back as he bends over (Illustration No. 21.)

It will be seen that this is a position for a "toss." The proper one here is the "long-distance toss." The "head-long toss" is also possible. Choice between the two sho8uld be made according to circumstances and the skill possessed by the defendant.

If the assailant intends to employ the "headlong-toss," the quick swing should be accomplished by a simultaneous release of both holds on the defendant's arm and thigh. The defendant may, at this point, enforce the "toss" by striking the floor with his feet at the moment he feels himself being lifted from the floor.

The "toss" or throw is accomplished by swinging aside the raised body of the defendant as the assailant

IL.21

gives a hitch forward in the manner in which a vicious horse disposes of his rider by indulging in an unexpected and vigorous kick.

The "toss" is augmented by the assailant's hold on the defendant's left arm and right thigh. By suddenly tightening and releasing this grasp with a quick jerk, considerable momentum is given to the defendant's body.

When properly executed, the "toss" will turn the defendant's body completely around over the back and "haunches" of the assailant, and the defendant, if he be a skilled Jiu-Jitsuian, will land on his feet.

The turning of the body in the "toss" may be compared to a wheel turning on its axis, the defendant's body being the wheel and the back and "haunches" of the assailant the axis. This explains the name given this operation, Koshi-Garuma, "Haunch-Wheel."

If the "headlong toss" be chosen, the quick swing should be accompanied by a sudden enforcement of the assailant's left arm which holds the defendant's left arm and the release of the hold on the defendant's thigh.

The strength required in operating the "human-wheel" is very great. It has been previously shown that the force exerted by the "haunches" plays an important part in Jiu-Jitsu method than for proving the efficacy of a "toss" or throw for the purpose of disabling a contestant.

In an actual fight, however, its effectiveness may be fully demonstrated. In such a case, it rests entirely with the assailant whether he will employ the "headlong toss" or not. So no matter what degree of skill the defendant may have attained, if the assailant be viciously inclined, he has it in his power to inflict a serious and perhaps fatal injury on the defendant.

Pericardium 2 or, "Heavenly Spring," is to be struck with your left elbow (Illustration No. 19) as you "wind in." This point is used in the treatment of cardiac pain and pain in the chest and back. Striking this point perpendicular to the left bicep will call the opponent's weight to shift to his left foot. This

achieves a vital principle in Jiu Jitsu of breaking the balance of the opponent.

The next move in this technique (Illustration No. 20), tells you to grab the right thigh of the opponent. Your elbow is also in good position to initiate a strike to Liver 13, or "Chapter Gate." This will further disrupt the balance of the opponent causing him to want to move away from the pain or discomfort.

P 2

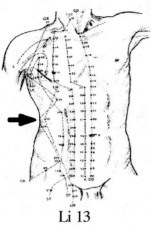

Li 13

For purposes of the technique, you are to strike the Liver 13 point with your elbow and then slap Gall Bladder 31, "Wind Market." The Liver and the Gall Bladder are paired organs in Traditional Chinese Medicine. The act of attacking both causes further disruption within the body, assisting you in completing the throw. Furthermore, if the opponent is incapcitated from either one or both of these attacks, it will be much harder for even an experience martial artist to break his fall.

GB 31

LESSON SEVEN

KE-KAISHI—"TURNING-BY-KICK."

In the operation of Ke-Kaishi, Offensive, the grapple is the familiar one in which the contestants grasp each other by one shoulder and one arm. The manner in which this hold is assumed is not essential, that is, it makes no difference whether the assailant uses his right hand to seize the defendant's left shoulder and his left to grasp his arm or reverses the order. The result will be the same in either case.

It is here (Illustration No 22) assumed that the assailant seizes the left shoulder of the defendant with his right hand and with his left hand grasps the defendant's right arm (Illustration No. 22) The defendant is at liberty to effect any grapple he desires, provided it be one that will not hinder the movements of both contestants (Illustration No. 22.)

When this grapple is effected, the assailant strides forward with his right foot (Illustration No. 22) and at the same time throws his weight with great force against the defendant's shoulders by means of his hold at that point. The assailant immediately follows this by a quick step back to his former position, accompanied by a swift turning of his body half way around the defendant's body (Illustration No. 23) which he effects by means of a stride with his left foot.

IL. 22

This action on the part of the assailant disturbs the defendant's balance (Illustration No. 23) and causes him to raise his left foot clear off the floor. While he is in the uncertain attitude and before he can determine his mode of resistance, the assailant delivers a kick with the heel of his right foot on the defendant's left knee (Illustration No. 23.) As the full force of the kick is felt by the defendant, the assailant pulls down on the defendant's left shoulder and pushes upward on his right arm (Illustration No. 23.) This is all that is needed to precipitate the defendant to the floor.

The assailant should take care to secure a firm footing after dealing the blow to the defendant's knee. The foot used in delivering the kick should regain the floor immediately so that the assailant may be in a position to proceed with the rest of the operation.

As the defendant's body falls to the floor, the assailant, still retaining his grapple on the defendant's arm and shoulder steps slightly backward out of the way of the defendant as he falls and when he is stretched at full length on the floor, the assailant releases his hold on the defendant's shoulder and with his hand thus freed, effects a grapple on the defendant's left scarf (Illustration No. 24.) While he holds the defendant down by this grapple at the scarf, the assailant slips his right hand down the defendant's left arm until the wrist is

reached (Illustration No. 24.)

Since the defendant's body falls to the floor on its side, one of his arms may be disabled by pressing it against the floor. The danger to the assailant of being "tossed" is not imminent so long as the assailant is able to keep the defendant on his side and prevent him from rolling on his back, thus freeing the entrapped arm (Illustration No. 24.)

IL. 23

As the assailant slips his hand down the defendant's arm to assume his grapple at the wrist, he steps backward with his left foot and with his right foot pressed close to the defendant's, rolls him over onto his side and then onto his face (Illustration No. 25.) This is accomplished by means of the start given by the assailant's right foot acting as

a lever and the grapple at the defendant's scarf.

As the assailant turns the defendant over face down on the floor (Illustration No. 25), he exchanges his grapple at the scarf for one on the left shoulder and draws the defendant's left arm backward over defendant's hips by means of his hold on the defendant's left wrist. As he does this he kneels on his right knee and with this knee over the defen-

IL. 24

dant's right shoulder, he can prevent him from rising or rolling by enforcing pressure of the knee and the grapple at the shoulder.

From this it will be seen that the "turning-down-by-kick" (Ke-Kaishi) calls for a nice perception and skill. The holds at the wrist and shoulder need to be carefully studied and practiced as it is by means of these two grapples that "submission" is to be enforced.

"Submission" may now be effected by the "armbreaking" process. In this instance it has a repulsive likeness to the method employed by a butcher in unjointing a fowl. In such a case it requires very little effort to effect the desired result, as a slight twist is all that is necessary to disjoint the members.

"Submission" is here fully effective by pressing

IL. 25

25

down on the defendant's shoulders and twisting his arm backward (Illustration No. 25) in the manner described.

Large Intestine 4 also known as, "Arm and Scapula," located at the end of the deltoid, where that muscle joins the bicep, is used when there is pain

LI 4

in the arm, shoulder, and rigidity in the neck. Conversely, it is also known to give "dead arm." When pressure from a strike or rub is applied, it can cause the shoulder to jump. It will cause the hips to go back and away from you. This lesson describes moving quickly in with a shove and then stepping back to your original position. This is still done, but with the opponent in some pain or discomfort. You do not have to return all the way to your original postion because your opponent will make some room for you as his hips drop back and away from you due to the Large Intestine 4 points.

The point kicked on the leg is Stomach 36. Known

as "Leg Three Miles", this point was known to treat tiredness in the legs, knee pain, etc. This is a valuable point in Traditional Chinese Medicine as well as martial arts. A kick diagonally up towards the inner thigh muscle will cause the knee to lock out, the hips to go back and the upper body to bend forward. Coupled with the Large Intentine points, this can make the throw easier to execute.

Front view of Leg

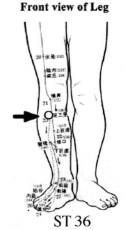

ST 36

In any self defense encounter, the element of surprise could be the difference between winning and losing or rather, living and dying. Remember, that this book was originally written to detail the techniques that were taught to the Japanese Army and Navy. This was not taught for sport, but for survival.

26

LESSON EIGHT

IRI-JIME—"SCARF-WRINGING."

The operation of Iri-Jime, "Scarf-Wringing," is one in which the offensive movements constitute a means of defense, an occurrence not unusual in Jiu-Jitsu. It has been explained heretofore that the operations embodied in Jiu-Jitsu were originally intended as a means of defense against sudden attack. Some of the means employed in the modernized methods are those used in the primitive form of Jiu-Jitsu and were originally applied only for defense, the offensive operations being of more recent invention, though even these are of ancient origin and have been in use among the Japanese for many hundreds of years.

In the operation of Iri-Jime, the defendant inaugurates the contest by seizing the assailant by the right scarf with his right hand and by the left scarf with his left hand. This crossing of the wrists constitutes a "neck-wringing" process (Illustration No. 26.)

The assailant remains perfectly passive, offering no resistance at all until the defendant begins to tighten his grasp in an effort to "wring" the assailant's neck. In doing this the defendant raises his arms and thus produces a space between them through which the assailant now quickly thrusts his left arm at the same time turning his body so that the defendant's arms are extended over the assailant's left shoulder (Illustration No. 27.)

IL. 26

Two important purposes are served by the assailant when he thrusts his arms between those of the defendant in the manner already described.

One of these is the wrenching off of the defendant's hold at the left scarf. This, the assailant accomplishes by forcing the assailant's rigid left arm slowly along the defendant's left arm from the shoulder to the elbow. The second advantage is that which the assailant can utilize by extending his arm as far as he can over the defendant's shoulder in wrenching off the defendant's grasp. When this has been done, the defendant's left arm is at the mercy of the assailant, who promptly proceeds to perform in the "winding-in" process.

IL. 27

27

To do this, the assailant hooks his left arm around the defendant's left arm and brings it under his own left arm. He also, with his right hand, grasps the defendant's right wrist and with these grapples effected proceeds to lift the defendant.

The contestants are now in the position shown in Illustration No. 27. The assailant throws his "haunches" against the defendant's abdomen with the intention of drawing the defendant across his back. The defendant is so closely held that he can offer no effectual resistance. With a sudden jerk, the assailant lifts the defendant and brings him to the position shown in Illustration No. 28.

As will be observed, there is but one method of disposing of the defendant's body poised across the assailant's stooping figure and that is by means of a "toss."

The same reasons that have heretofore dictated the choice of the two available "tosses" hold good in this case, the "side-toss" being preferable to the "headlong-toss" on account of inflicting less injury to the defendant.

IL. 28

The "side-toss" having been chosen by the assailant as a means of disposing of his burden, he throws the defendant to the ground by a sudden lift of his shoulder and a release of the right-hand grapple.

It is possible, however, to effect a "submission" if the assailant so desires. If such be the case, the assailant tightens his hold on the defendant's right wrist and by straightening up, allows the defendant to slide down his back to the floor. The assailant follows the sliding body by bending backward until the defendant is stretched at full length on the floor, when he kneels beside the defendant and proceeds to effect "submission" by means of the "arm-breaking" process, Which has been fully described in previous lessons.

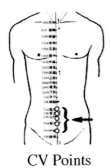

CV Points

The idea behind any toss, is to first break the opponent's balance. Failure to do so can put your welfare in jeopardy. You will notice as in IL. 27, the person initiating the throw, first backs into his opponent. He thrusts his hips in the Conception vessel points (See Lesson 2) shown in the CV Points diagram. These points will assist in breaking the balance of your opponent so that you can complete the throw, with his "assistance, " and follow up with the same "submission" as in earlier Lessons.

28

LESSON NINE

KAKE-AI—"MEETING-BY-HANGING."

In the operation of Kake-Ai, the initiatory grapples of the assailant are effected by seizing with his right hand the defendant's left arm and with his left hand grasping the defendant's scarf (Illustration No. 29.) The defendant may effect any grapple he desires, provided it does not hamper the movements of both contestants. It is here assumed that the defendant's grapple is similar to that of the assailant (Illustration No. 29.)

IL. 29

In this position each of the contestants strives by alternate efforts of pushing and pulling to gain the advantage. This continues until the assailant gives a shove to the defendant that, for the moment, makes him lose his balance. As this is accomplished the assailant seizes the opportunity to sway the defendant backward and forward by means of his grapple at the scarf and arm of the defendant. This creates a momentum, which the assailant utilizes for his own benefit.

Taking a step forward with his left foot to the left of the assailant's left foot (Illustration No. 30), the assailant braces his left leg against the defendant's left leg and by means of the initiatory grapples and by bending or leaning to the right, draws the defendant's body with his (Illustration No. 31) and swings the defendant to the floor in front of him (Illustration No. 32.)

IL. 30

This requires very little exertion on the part of the assailant. No more in fact than is used by the assailant to draw his own body over with the weight of the defendant's body resisting this effort. The position of the assailant's foot here prevents the defendant from regaining his balance and offering resistance.

The significance of the name Kake-Ai, "Meeting-by-Hanging," is here explained, the fall of the defendant being accomplished as the assailant "hangs" on the scarf and arm of the defendant.

The left hip of the assailant, as it is thrust against the defendant's side (Illustration No. 31) in this position is a source of considerable power in effecting the "meeting-by-hanging" which is controlled by the assailant's

29

grapple.

The defendant's body shall fall to the floor on its back. The assailant accomplishes this by turning the upper part of his body and imparting a rolling motion to the defendant's body as he swings it to the floor by means of "hanging" to the defendant. If the assailant is possessed of sufficient skill he may cause the defendant to the fall in front of him so that he will not have to change his footing in effecting "submission."

As the defendant's body comes to the floor, the assailant stoops enough to maintain his grapple, which may now be exchanged for the hold to be used in enforcing "submission."

IL. 31

The left hand that holds the scarf is now shifted to a grasp on the defendant's left arm and this in turn gives way to a hold on the wrist on the same arm.

The defendant bending over the assailant as he lies on his back applies his left foot as a lever under the assailant's hip and turns him on his side (Illustration No. 30.) he then kneels on the defendant with his left knee and releases the grapple of his right hand on defendant's scarf, bracing the defendant's left shoulder and is now ready to enforce "submission" by means of an "arm-breaking" process.

The "submission" is effected by bending defendant's left arm over the assailant's left knee by means of the pressure applied at the wrist, while the assailant with his right arm is bearing down on the defendant's left shoulder.

IL. 32

By this means "submission" is fully effective. The process here employed is very similar to one described in a previous lesson. The chief point of difference is the introduction here of the hold on the shoulder. This forcing down of the shoulder, instead of the chin or neck, is merely to hold the defendant's body on its side and does not in any manner aid in affecting "submission."

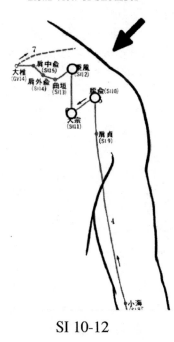

Rear view of Shoulder

SI 10-12

In simple terms...this is a hip toss followed up by another arm bar. The significance of the Small Intestine points employed before the act of "submisson," are more important than the author had let on.

We will begin by explaining the merits of each point. In a confrontation, the accuracy to target these points does take some degree of proficiency and that is why we have chosen three relevant points that are in close proximity to each other.

Small Intestine 10 sits on the upper part fo the rear deltoid, approximately where the shoulder joins the scapula. It is used to assist in healing when there is pain and weakness in the shoulder and arm, therefore, it can be a tool for creating pain and weakness in the shoulder and arm.

Small instestine 11 lies in the middle of the upper third of the middle third of the scapula. It is used to relieve pain in the scapular region as well as the elbow, arm, and treat the symptoms of asthma.

Again, this tells us that if we can treat these symptoms with this point, then we can cause them. This point is also in the lung region which can cause of spasming of the lungs and can cause the opponent breathing difficulty.

Small Intestine 12 sits directly above Small Intestine 11 in a depression on the scapula when the arm is raised. This point is used in the treatment of motor impairment of the shoulder and arm, thereby telling us that it will cause the same problems when used for purposes of "submisson."

As a side note, I have personally used this group of points as well as having been on the receiving end. The beauty of this area is that you can quickly find one or more as you drop your knee, or use your arm and your body weight will assist to hold the opponent down.

LESSON TEN

MAWARI-GACHI — "WINNING-BY-ROUNDING."

In the operation of Mawari-Gachi, the grapple effected by the assailant is one that has long since become familiar to the student of Jiu-Jitsu, viz. the hold of one contestant on the outstretched arms on the other.

In this instance, it is assumed that the assailant grasps the right sleeve of the defendant with his left hand, and the left sleeve of the defendant with his right hand (Illustration No. 33.)

The grapple of the defendant may be effected in the same manner (Illustration No. 33.)

In this position, the two strive on against each other for an advantage, which is perceived by the assailant at the moment the defendant retreats with his right foot or strides forward with his left foot to strengthen and brace himself for the attack of the assailant. It makes no difference whether the defendant puts his right foot forward or his left foot back, or vice-versa, but it is here assumed that his right foot is to the rear and his left foot forward (Illustration No. 33.)

IL. 33

The assailant, with a sudden shove on the defendant's arms, now raises his right foot and places it against the defendant's left knee (Illustration No. 33), at the same time turning himself half-way around and falling backward to the floor (Illustration No. 34.)

This action, of course, pulls the defendant over (Illustration No. 35), and, as the assailant falls further back and rests on his back, he has the defendant in position to effect a "toss."

It will be observed that the assailant has kept his foot braced against he defendant's knee and has used it as a lever by which to swing himself around the defendant.

It is upon this action of "rounding" himself about the defendant, that the name of the operation herein described is based.

A very nice skill on the part of the assailant is required for effecting the position, which brings him to the point shown in Illustration No. 35.

IL. 34

The intention of the assailant to throw the defendant by means of a "toss" is now apparent. It will also be observed that the exertion on the part of the defendant in drawing back in order to maintain his balance as the assailant falls backward, is to be utilized by the assailant in effecting the "toss."

The "headlong" toss is the one by means of which the assailant intends to dispose of the defendant. The latter, perceiving the outcome, may elect to enforce the "toss" by kicking the floor as he is about to be thrown.

By kicking the defendant's right foot from under him and enforcing his right foot against the defendant's left knee, the assailant throws the defendant over his head. The latter, if he be a skilled Jiu-Jitsuian will land on his feet and side.

The "arm-toss" can be only imperfectly effected here, as it would, in all probability, bring the defendant's body over on the chest or abdomen of the assailant and enable him to enforce a "submission" on the assailant.

IL. 35

The "side-toss" would present the same difficulty, for the defendant would be able to renew the attack before the assailant could regain his feet.

The assailant, as he throws the defendant over his head by means of the "headlong toss" should release his grapples and spring to his feet by means of the momentum created by the "toss."

No "submission" is to be effected here, the "toss" is termination of the contest.

Let us now explore the leg point that Dr. Kikuta used for this technique. It was used to brace the leg of the opponent as a precursor to a throw. There is more that should be explained about the use of this point, along with some others that can be of great use to execute this throw.

Front view of Leg

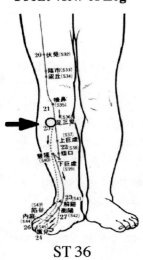

ST 36

Stomach 36 or "Leg Three Miles," is the point that is referred to in this lesson. Legend has it that this point was used by the chinese army centuries ago when the foot soldiers began to tire during their marches. They would stop, slap this point, massage it vigorously, and be strong enough to march another "three miles."

Along with functioning as an excellent point for local maladies (knee), Stomach 36 is great for motor impairment of the legs and lower back pain. Again, this tells us that since this point can assist in healing these areas of affliction, it can be used to cause temporary or even long term harm to these areas.

Dr. Kikuta uses this point to brace his foot against as he executes the throw. This point can also be kicked quite strongly to break the opponent's balance and cause his upper body to bend forward. In this position, the opponent is much easier to throw. "Submission" may not always result in the throw, but temporary malfunction fo the knee can definately end the contest.

Outside view of Leg

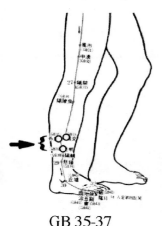

GB 35-37

There are additional points that can be used to assist in this throw. The Gall Bladder meridian runs from the top of the head to the outside edge of the foot.

Gall Bladder 35-37 sit on the outside edge of the leg inbetween the knee and ankle. This is an area that responds very well to striking. Not only does it cause problems with the knee, but with the ankle as well. All three of these points are use to promote knee health. Once again this tells us that it can be used to facilitate problems within that area, thus causing imbalance as well.

LESSON ELEVEN

SEOE-NAGE—"TOSSING-OVER-BACK."

In the operation of Seoe-Nage, the grapples may be effected in the usual manner, the assailant grasping the defendant's arms and the defendant holding the assailant's arms.

It is here assumed, that the assailant grasps the defendant's left arm with his right hand and the right arm with his left hand, the defendant's having the reverse of this position. Holding each other in the manner described, the two strive for an advantage which is presented to the assailant when the defendant gives him a harder shove than usual, thus relaxing the assailant's left arm which enables him to free it and effect another grapple.

It not infrequently happens that the assailant finds it very difficult to free this left arm. Especially will this be the case when the defendant possesses superior strength. The assailant will then have to resort to the strategetic move of relaxing his own hold in order to distract the defendant's attention, when by suddenly twisting his arm to and fro he may wrench off the defendant's grasp.

IL. 36

IL. 37

As the assailant perceives the opening he strides forward placing his left foot between the feet of the defendant, at the same time slipping back his right foot so that he makes a tremendous stride (Illustration No. 36.)

He then raises his right arm above his head (Illustration No. 36.) and thrusts his head under his upraised arm and that of his adversary, drawing the latter close to him by means of his grapple on the defendant's left arm, while with his free arm he grasps the defendant around the left thigh. This brings the contestants to the position shown in Illustration No. 37, though the manner of the grapple by means of the assailant's left arm cannot be seen in the illustration.

In this position the assailant is ready to lift the defendant by pressing his left side and "haunches" against the defendant's abdomen, giving a quick swing to the left and upward as he draws down on the left arm, and lifting the defendant by means of the grapple

35

on the left thigh, he brings him to a horizontal position across his back (Illustration No. 38.)

Either the "headlong toss" or the "side-toss" may be chosen to dispose of the defendant. If it be the former, the defendant should kick in order to enforce the "toss," so that he may turn headlong in the air and feet first without injury to himself.

IL. 38

IL. 39

The "side-toss" may be employed here, although it is more difficult to accomplish than the "headlong toss."

When the defendant comes to the floor by means of a "side-toss" the assailant bends over him (Illustration No. 39) and holds him down on the floor with his left hand, which he presses firmly against the defendant's chest (Illustration No. 39.) He then effects a grapple with which to enforce "submission." This can be explained in previous lessons.

When the "headlong toss" is employed no "submission" is effected.

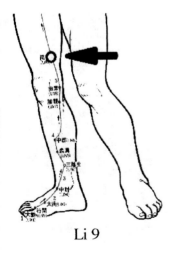

Li 9

Liver 9 is is a very sensative point located on the inside of the leg and sits in close proximity to the femoral arter, vein, and nerve. This point, when struck, pinched or pressed, can affect the stability of the opponent. There is a chain reaction effect when this is done. Above , the hip startes to collapse. Below, the knee and ankle begin to give out. This is an excellent point with which to assist the throw, once the upper body is secured.

LESSON TWELVE

UMENOEDA-ORI – "BREAKING-OF-THE-PLUM-BRANCH."

In this operation the grapples are effected by each contestant grasping the belt of the other with both hands.

It is assumed that the assailant seizes the defendant's back belt with his right hand, his right are passing over the defendant's left arm, while with his left hand he grasps the defendant's side belt, his left arm passing under the defendant's right arm (Illustration N. 40). The defendant may assume his grapples in the same manner, his position, of course, being the reverse of the assailant's.

IL. 40

IL. 41

Maintaining these grapples, the contestants strive against each other until an opening is presented to the assailant when the defendant takes a stride forward with his left foot thus approaching the assailant's right foot (Illustration No. 40).

At this moment the assailant gives a sudden push to the defendant in order to ascertain whether latter's footing is secure. Upon finding that it is, he immediately releases the hold maintained with his left hand on the defendant's belt and thrusts his left arm over the left arm of the defendant (Illustration No. 41). At the same time he stoops and takes a stride backward with his left foot.

In this stooping position the assailant's back is exposed to an attack from the defendant's right hand and he must therefore proceed with all possible speed to avail the impending danger. He should conceal his intention from the defendant until it is too late for the latter to take advantage of the opportunity thus afforded.

The assailant's next move is to wind his left arm around the defendant's left arm thus wrenching off the defendant's hold on the assailant's side belt by stooping still lower and forcing the entrapped arm of the defendant under his own.

When he has freed himself from this grasp of the defendant, he extends his left arm between the defendant's legs and takes hold of the defendant's left leg just below the knee (Illustration No. 42). While the assailant has been securing this hold, he has also taken the precaution to shift his feet

IL. 42

until he has effected a wide stride and has his left foot between the defendant's thus bringing his left thigh under the defendant's body (Illustration No. 42).

In this position with his left "haunch" almost against the defendant's abdomen, the assailant has but to straighten up and lift up on the defendant's left leg to bring the latter off the floor and to balance him on his "haunches", preliminary to letting him slide to the floor (Illustration No. 43). If the

IL. 43

latter maintains his grapple on the assailant's back belt with his right hand, the assailant should kneel as the body falls, so that the defendant will be unable to pull him backward. The defendant's body should be so controlled that it will land with the right leg between the assailant's feet (Illustration No. 43).

The assailant now effects the grapples with which he is to exact "submission". Standing over the defendant, as shown in Illustration No. 43, he grasps the defendant's left leg below the knee with his left hand, and, with his right hand, takes hold of the foot near the toes.

He then sits down upon the defendant's right thigh and drawn the entrapped leg over his left knee. The assailant now slips his left hand and arm

IL. 44

under the defendant's entrapped leg and grasps his own right wrist (Illustration No. 44). In this position he is able to effect "submission" by means of the "leg-breaking" process, a slight twist to the left being sufficient to cause intense pain.

It is from this twisting or bending, which is supposed to resemble the breaking of the branch of a tree, that the operation takes its name.

The principal of the "leg-breaking" process is the same as that involved in the "arm-braking" process described in previous lessons and "submission" may be rendered fully effective by its use.

The pictures above demonstrate the "submission" technique. I feel that more should be discussed about the finer points of each technique to give the practitioner more chance for success. Dr. Kikuta has spoken many times

Top view of foot

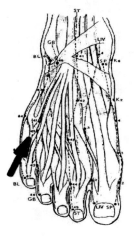

GB 41-42

about how an experienced Jiu-Jitsuian would react or respond, but without elaborating on the points necessary to become more experienced. It is sort of a "catch 22."

Gall Bladder 41 sits on the outside of the foot in between the 4th and 5th metatarsal. This point sits in a similar position to the Triple Warmer 3 point on the hand. It is used to treat pain and spasm in the foot and toes. The Gall Bladder Meridian travels from the top of the head to the foot and is used in the treatment of many maladies that the body may encounter. GB 41 is used to treat many illnesses that can occur in the upper body in addition to problems that may occur in the general area of the point.

Gall Bladder 42 is located in the same depression just an inch or so from GB 41 in the direction of the toes. This point has a similar function as the previous one, and in addition, it is used in the treatment of tinitus, thus telling us that it may disrupt the hearing of the opponent.

When pressure is applied to the foot in the manner described above in Illustration 44, intense pain can be felt by the opponent. The technique is further aided by sitting on the opponent's thigh. The Gall Bladder Meridian runs up the thigh. The pain is increased two ways; by the weight of your body sitting on the thigh as you apply torque, and by the additional stimulation of the Gall Bladder Meridian further up the body on the thigh.

LESSON THIRTEEN

ADVANCED KOTE-GAISHI – "HAND-TURNING"

In this operation the defendant approaches the assailant with one hand clinched and extended. It does not make any difference whether it be the right or left hand which is presented to the assailant in this manner, but it is assumed here that the defendant extends his left hand to the assailant (Illustration No. 45) and that the latter grasps it with his right, pressing his thumb in between the knuckles of the defendant's hand and grasping the defendant's palm with his fingers.

By the means of this grasp, the assailant is able to inflict severe pain on the defendant and when he presses on the back of the defendant's hand with his thumb and draws him forward, the defendant will involuntarily step forward in order to avoid the pain. This gives the assailant the opportunity he is seeking and when the defendant's left foot is advanced (Illustration No. 45) the assailant raises his right arm, thus twisting the defendant's left arm.

IL. 45

The pain thus produced distracts the defendant's mind, so that he is not as careful to avoid the assailant as he should be. This neglect gives the assailant the opportunity to kick the defendant's left knee with his left foot (Illustration No. 46), and, at the same time he twists the defendant's left arm and draws it further toward him.

The defendant may attempt to resist the assailant's efforts to twist his arm by turning his body in the same direction that the assailant twists his arm and by raising himself on his toes, but when he does so he will be contributing to his own defeat, as this exertion will be turned by the assailant to his own account.

While the kicking of the foot and the drawing aside of the defendant's arm are sufficient to cause the defendant's body to fall on the floor there is still another means of obtaining this result. This is afforded the assailant when he extends his left arm and with his left hand presses the right cheek, or the right side of the defendant's neck, thus forcing the defendant's head to one side with considerable force.

IL. 46

As the defendant's body slides to the floor from the force of the impact of the assailant's left foot on the defen-

40

dant's left knee, the assailant draws his left foot out of the way and releases his grapple. By hooking his foot around the defendant's knee the assailant may guide the defendant's body so that it will fall on its back.

This process requires very little actual exertion and yet by means of the movements herein described a man of more than ordinary strength may be overcome.

If the defendant should effect a grapple on the assailant's left arm (Illustration No. 46) and maintain it after he is thrown, the assailant will have to follow the falling body to the floor by stooping and then exact a "submission" by means of an "arm-breaking" process.

Advanced Kote-Gaishi, it will be observed, is an improved method of Kote-Gaishi. The "hand-turning" in this instance is done with one hand, while in Kote-Gaishi both hands are used, and much of the exertion of the latter operation is eliminated.

Unless the defendant maintains is grapple the falling of the assailant's body terminates the contest, no "submission" being effected.

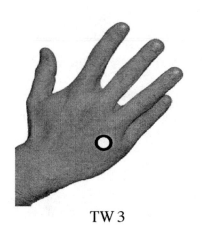

TW 3

Triple Warmer 3 sits between the fourth and fifth metacarpal bones, just below the knuckles of the pinky and ring finger. Since many of the points of the Triple Warmer meridian affect the ear, it is safe to say that these points also affect the balance of your opponent. As breaking the balance of your opponent is a key component to gaining an advantage in grappling situations, points of the Triple Warmer meridian are excellent tools to use.

There are many styles of martial arts that include this technique as a part of their arsenal. The arrows included in the wrist action of Fig. A, show the proper torque that is necessary to achieve maximum effectivenss with minimum effort to drop your opponent to the floor. This wrist action is prevalent in Wally Jay's Small Circle Jujitsu system.

Fig. A

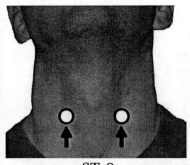

ST. 9

In Illustration No. 46, the author refers to pressing on the cheek or the side of the defendant's neck. There are few points in question here that need to be clarified to add to the overall effectiveness of the technique.

Stomach 9 ("Man's Prognosis") sits in direct proximity to the carotid sinus...a blood pressure monitor, inbetween the sternocleidomastoid muscle and the wind pipe, approximately one third up the neck from the collar bone. When pressed in and down the body of the opponent will turn in the direction of the pressure to escape the hold.

Small Intestine 18 ("Zygoma Crevice") is a point on the cheek that works well with wrist lock. When you insert your thumb underneath the cheek bone, as if you were pushing through the skull, the opponent will jerk his head backwards, thus aiding you in completing the throw on the wrist. You have broken your opponents balance, and in the process, exposed his back to the floor. With pressure applied properly on the wrist, he falls to the

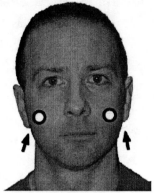

SI 18

floor and you are prepared to apply a "submission" if it is neccesary.

LESSON FOURTEEN

KATA-GURUMA – "SHOULDER-WHEEL"

As the contestants approach each other in this operation, the assailant grasps the wrist of the defendant. It does not matter which hand he uses to effect this grapple, although it is here assumed that he seizes the defendant's left wrist with his left hand (Illustration No. 47). In this position, the two strive against each other watching for an opening, the defendant hoping to free himself from the assailant's grasp, and the assailant striving to maintain his hold in order to carry out his original intention. This he does by striding to and fro and bewildering the defendant who tries to free his arm and effect a closer grapple.

IL. 47

After a time the defendant perceives that it is useless to persist in the effort to free his arm and raises his right arm (Illustration No, 47) with the intention of delivering a blow on the assailant's chest with his fist. This resistance, as is usual in Jui-Jitsu, is utilized by the assailant for his own benefit, and, in this instance, is just what the assailant has been awaiting.

As the defendant raises his fist, the assailant thrusts up his left arm and thus uses the defendant's own arm to protect himself from the defendant's blow. Before the defendant can make another thrust, the assailant swings his body around sidewise and places his right hip against the defendant's left side (Illustration No, 48), at the same time thrusting his right arm, which he holds rigid, under the defendant's extended right arm (Illustration No. 48) and then over the defendant's left shoulder (Illustration No. 49).

IL. 48

This brings the assailant to a position where he can protect himself from any attack planned by the defendant to be operated by means of his right hand.

The right hand of the assailant is now at the back of the defendant's neck and capable of enforcing pressure at this point. The assailant's right side and chest are exposed to the defendant in this position but he is able to protect himself from any attack from the defendant by holding him as far away as possible by means of his extended right arm.

The assailant, it will be observed, holds the defendant's left arm in an "arm-breaking" position. By pulling down on the arm by means of his hold of the wrist and by straightening his own right arm, the assailant may cause the defendant to suffer intense pain. By means of the pressure which he can apply at the back of the defendant's neck and the "arm-breaking" hold "submission" may be effected.

IL. 49

The name Kata-Guruma, "Shoulder-Wheel", does not seem to have any especial significance as none of the movement herein described bringing into play any great amount of strength derived from the shoulder. The name probably owes its origin to the fact that formerly this operation was included among those in which the shoulder force instead of the "haunch" force was chiefly employed.

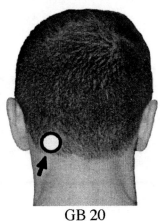

GB 20

Gall Bladder 20, or "Wind Pond," is another great point to gain control of the opponent's head. The angle and direction, as shown in the diagram, is in and up towards the opposite eye.

The term pond or pool refers to a gathering of energy or chi. If this explanation is not suitable to western minds, then the local anatomy with regards to western medicine is the Occipital Foramen.

This point is used in acupuncture to treat head ache and dizziness. Using this point in self defense situations can possibly cause the same maladies that it helps to cure.

UDE-NO-MA – "UNDER THE-ARM"

In this operation, the initiatory grapple is effected by the assailant as he seizes the defendant's left wrist. In order that the defendant may not effect a grapple, which is essential to the assailant's success, the latter should keep well away from the defendant by rapidly striding to and fro. This will bewilder the defendant and render him more liable to attack as the opening is presented.

IL. 50

The assailant perceives his opportunity as the defendant steps forward with his left foot or retreats with his right foot; and the assailant strides forward with his left foot (Illustration No. 50) or with his right foot. Immediately following these movements the assailant takes a long step to the left side of the defendant and raises the latter's left arm by means of the grapple at the wrist. With his left hand he effects a second grapple on his right arm just above the elbow (Illustration No. 50).

Making a pivot of his left foot, the assailant turns himself toward the right until he stands at the left side of the defendant and behind him as shown in Illustration No. 51.

It is from this movement that the name Ude-No-Ma, "Under –the-Arm", is derived.

IL. 51

Up to this point, the arm of the defendant has been grasped so that there could be no slipping either at the wrist or at the elbow, and it is now held in such a position as to be twisted almost clear around.

It will be observed that there is a moment during the turning of the assailant when his back is fully exposed to the defendant, but it is presumed that the pain that the assailant is able to inflict by means of the twisting position in which

he holds the defendant's arm, as well as the fact that he turns very quickly before the defendant has an opportunity to take advantage of the situation and offer an effectual resistance to the assailant's attack, combine to render an attack impossible. The twisting which the assailant gives to the defendant's left arm, is accomplished quite as much by his turning as he steps behind the defendant as it is by the force of the grapples on the defendant's arm.

IL. 52

The only way in which the defendant is able to protect himself from this twisting is by turning in unison with the assailant's body, but in order to do this he has to stoop forward. This action is immediately utilized by the assailant for his own benefit. Standing by the defendant the assailant kicks the left foot of his adversary with his right foot, accompanying the kick by forcing down the defendant by means of the grapples on his arm. This causes the defendant to fall to the floor (Illustration No. 52).

The defendant now lies upon the floor while the assailant maintains his initiatory grapples unaltered. As the defendant falls, the assailant kneels beside him (Illustration No. 52) with his right knee capable of enforcing pressure upon the defendant's back.

The twisting position in which the defendant's left arm is held is the one by means of which the defendant exacts "submission".

As will be observed in Illustration No. 52, "submission" is to be exacted by means of an "arm-breaking" process which is here fully effective.

TW 10

You will notice that the Triple Warmer Rub point is again being used, not only to set up the technique, but to bring about "submission." There is talk about the grapple with the wrist, but that will not do anyting until this point is applied in the proper manner.

When you place your left arm under the arm of the opponent, you are to roll your arm slightly back towards you while pulling through the arm (see Illustration No. 50). This breaks your opponent's balance allowing you to step under him and use the same point to bring your opponent down to the floor.

At this point you have a couple of options; if the opponent falls to the floor by the arm bar alone, then you can move to "submission" immediately. If your oppoenent has the ability to resist, or the arm bar was applied incorrectly, then you can kick the opponent's leg out from under him with a right leg back kick. This is not a kick that is applied with the bottom of the foot, but rather with the

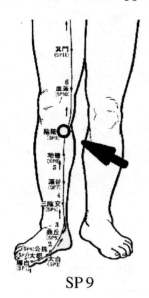

SP 9

calf / back of the leg to a point called Spleen 9 ("Yin Mound Spring).

Spleen 9 is located on the interior aspect of the leg, and below the knee. The angle and direction to affect this point is through the leg and up towards the outside part of the leg, just above the knee. If you draw an X acros the knee, you will have the angle and direction to attack the knee from four different points of view.

One of the functions of Spleen 9 is to treat pain in the knee, thereby telling us that we can cause the knee to release with the proper kick, with the proper force, with the proper angle and direction.

Points that are usually located above or below a joint work well combined with grappling techniques that are designed to take advantage when attacking these areas.

Bladder 23 ("Kidney Back Transporting Point") is a warning point for the Kidney. Whenever pressure is placed on warning points, the body reacts accordingly. "Submission" becomes easier when using points such as these, but not guaranteed.

Bladder 23 is an extremely potent point. It is used to treat everything from lower back pain, to weakness of the knee, to blurred vision, dizziness, deafness, asthma, and diarrhea. From this list, one can assume that this point is an excellent tool to aid in "submission."

BL 23

LESSON SIXTEEN

UKI-AI—"OPERATING-IN-WALKING."

In this operation, the distinctive feature is that no grapples are to be effected in the preliminary movements. The two contestants simply walk side by side until the opening is presented which it is at the moment the assailant and defendant step forward simultaneously with the right foot or with the left foot. Both defendant and assailant have an equal chance to effect the initiatory grapple.

IL. 53

It is here assumed that the opening is presented as the contestants stride forward with their respective left feet. The assailant then seizes the defendant's left wrist, pressing the thumb of his right hand against the back of the defendant's left hand, while his fingers extend across the palm of the grappled hand (Illustration No. 53).

The seizure of the defendant's wrist inaugurates the operation. The assailant raises the arm he has seized, and, with his left hand, effects a second grapple on the defendant's wrist (Illustration No. 54). This hold on the defendant's left hand with the assailant's two hands is very similar to the "turning-down" hold in Kote Gaishi.

IL. 54

The next movement of the assailant is to twist the entrapped arm with a circular motion, the shoulder being the center of the circle and the wrist in its movement describing the circle's circumference (Illustration No. 55). This action may be compared to the winding of a clock.

As the entrapped arm is thus twisted until it very nearly describes a complete circle, the assailant is compelled to turn his head and the upper part of his body in the direction of the twisting. This interferes with the defendant's equilibrium, and, the assailant perceiving this, raises his left foot and applies it at the back of the defendant's left knee (Illustration No. 55). By means of the pressure thus exerted the assailant prevents the defendant from regaining his balance either by turning the upper part of his body or shoving his right foot back.

In this position the assailant draws downward and aside on the defendant's wrist on which he has a "turning-down" grapple. He leans forward as he forcibly presses on the back of the defendant's knee, thus augmenting the backward fall. The defendant's body should be guided in the air so that it will fall on its back (Illustration No. 56).

IL. 55

As the defendant comes to the floor, the assailant kneels on his right knee, retaining the "turning-down" hold as it was effected in the initiatory grapple (Illustration No. 56). In this attitude, the assailant can at any time enforce "submission."

The "turning-down" hold is exactly adapted to the "wrist-breaking" process. The upper arm of the defendant is pressed close against the floor and the wrist may be bent inward by a pressure of the assailant's thumbs on the back of the defendant's hand.

Usually this is all that is required in enforcing "submission." But in case the defendant should attempt to resist, the assailant's left knee may be enforced against the defendant's chest to hold him down while the knee pressure is being applied.

In this position the defendant's wrist could be broken before he could rise with the intention of renewing the attack.

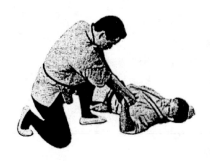

IL. 56

TW 3

Notice that the Triple Warmer 3 point is again being used. Refer to lesson 13, Fig. A. From my personal experience with this technique, I would never raise the opponent's hand as far from the origin of the technique. When you use too much movement to apply any technique, you not only give the opponent ample time to escape, but allow too much of his body to be able to resist. If the technique was applied and torque was immediately applied, then the rate of success would be greater.

I would surmise that the in order to make the technique more apparent, the movement was exaggerated for purposes of this book..

Rear view of leg

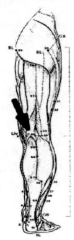

BL 40

Bladder 40 ("Supporting the Middle"), some acupuncture systems refer to this point as Bladder 54, is the same point that we used when we were younger on our friends and one that children are still using today. The angle and direction on this point is in and down. Motor impairment of the hip joint and lower extremeties are two properties that make this a great point for self defense.

When this point is used in conjunction with the wrist grapple, the rate of succes for the take down goes up dramatically. Remember though, their is no substitute for good technique.

LESSON SEVENTEEN

TENGU — "GOBLIN'S GRIP."
ATE — "Vital Touch."

One of the most interesting and also the most effective operations in Jiu-Jitsu is Tengu or "Goblin's Grip."

Unlike most other Jiu-Jitsu operations, it is an Offensive instead of a Defensive method. In Japan it is used chiefly by the policemen and detectives in capturing criminals of all sorts when they attempt resist arrest.

Detectives and policemen in Japan are appointed, not on account of superior size or strength, but in accordance with their attainments in Jiu-Jitsu. To those who are especially skilled in Tengu, the preference is given.

When a candidate for admission to the staff of detectives or to the police force presents himself before the authorities for examination, he is required to show his own methods of tying and roping. From this it will be seen that he must have devoted considerable time to the study and practice of this art. He is expected to be able to capture even the most desperate criminal single-handed and without resource to weapons of any sort.

The name Tengu, or "Goblin's Grip" is derived from the idea that the assailant shows almost superhuman power in overcoming his adversary.

When a Jiu-Jitsuian desires to operate by means of Tengu, He advances behind his adversary within grappling distance, and, kneeling behind him, grasps an ankle in each hand (Illustration No. 57).

IL. 57

This is for the purpose of pulling the defendant's feet from under him and thus precipitating him to the floor. If the defendant be walking or running, less force will be required to trip him than if he were standing still when the attack is made. In the latter case, a sudden backward pull will be necessary.

As the defendant falls, his endeavor to land on his hands and feet, instead of his abdomen, is met and counteracted by the action of the assailant, who places his right hand on the defendant's back (Illustration No. 58) and holds him down by means of this grapple and one which he takes with his left hand on the defendant's left leg (Illustra-

IL. 58

tion No. 58).

At the precise moment the defendant exchanges this position, by means of a quick spring, for a seat astride the assailant's body (Illustration No. 59). With the defendant's legs stretched out straight and his abdomen touching the floor, there is no chance for him to turn so as to throw the assailant off his back.

IL. 59

The assailant is now in position to administer a "vital touch" to his opponent. This he does by striking the defendant's head at the side just back of the ears (V. t, Fig 1, Chart) with his open palms (Illustration No. 59).

The force of this blow is very slight and if it were given at any other part of the body would hardly be felt. Its effect, here is to produce dizziness amounting in some cases to unconsciousness, much depending on the force of the blow and the susceptibility of the victim to such a "touch."

Another by more painful method of disabling the defendant at this point is available by the assailant when he has taken his seat astride the prostrate body. Extending his left hand over the defendant's left shoulder, he seizes his chin, and, then, with his

IL. 60

right hand at the back of the defendant's head, he forces the head aside, while with the left hand he lifts it up (Illustration No. 60).

As this "neck-twisting" process is enforced, the assailant's left forearm rests on the defendant's left shoulder. By means of this pressure and the enforcement of the assailant's left knee, the defendant at this point is prevented from offering effectual resistance.

The "vital touch" does not inflict permanent injury and is almost painless, but the "neck-twisting" process is capable of causing intense pain.

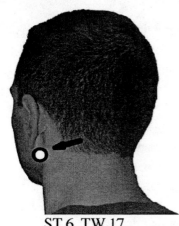

Stomach 6 and Triple Warmer 17 are in such close proximity, one diagram has been used for the purpose of this add on information to this technique.

Stomach 6 ("Jaw Chariot") sits at the corner of the jaw. The angle and direction needed to affect this point is towards the opponent's chin.

Triple Warmer 17 ("Heaven's Appearance") is located in the depression behind the jaw, below the ear lobe. This point needs pressure in and up towards the top of the skull for maximum effectiveness.

ST 6, TW 17

When the area, that these points are located in is struck, you will hit both. Though the angle and direction is different for each point, you will affect both nonetheless. Each point can cause dizziness and or unconciousness, depending on force and intent. Both points sit close to the facial nerve and can cause some temporary facial paralysis so caution is suggested.

M-HN 18 has been discussed in prior lessons. This point is used to release the sternocleidomastoid muscles in the neck, and a neck break or "submisson" can be achieved with limited pressure and or strength.

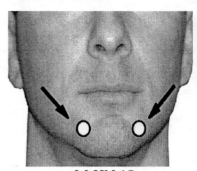

M-HN 18

LESSON EIGHTEEN

UDE-HISHIGI — "ARM-BREAKING."

The object of this operation is to obtain a "submission" position while the contestants are standing.

The initiatory grapples are effected by the assailant seizing the defendant's wrist, it being assumed here that the defendant's left wrist is grasped by the assailant's left hand (Illustration No. 61).

The assailant, who desires to have his right hand free to carry out his plan of attack, endeavors to keep as far away as possible from the defendant's free right arm with which he might effect a grapple and thus interfere with the assailant's plan.

IL. 61

IL. 62

IL. 63

The position in which the contestants stand (Illustration No. 61) is such as would enable the assailant to shield himself from the blow from the assailant's right fist by raising or lowering the grappled arm.

Standing in the position shown in Illustration No,. 61, the assailant strides forward swinging his left foot around on the pivot made by his right foot (Illustration No. 62), extends his right arm over the defendant's left shoulder and seizes his opponent's left scarf (Illustration No. 62). This is followed by raising the defendant's arm by means of the grapple at the wrist (Illustration No. 62), and the thrusting of the assailant's head under the arm thus raised (Illustration No. 63).

In the initiatory grapples, the assailant placed his thumb between the defendant's knuckles and this hold, when rigidly made and retained, is exactly adapted for holding the arm across the assailant's shoulders when he thrusts his head under the extended arm (Illustration No. 63).

In the position shown in Illustration No. 63 the assailant has but to pull down the defendant's wrist to effect an "arm-breaking" hold.

Another method of effecting "submission" while standing may be operated by the defendant who first seizes the assailant's right wrist with his right hand as shown

IL. 64

IL. 65

in Illustration N. 64. This grapple, as in the previous case, leaves a free arm to the defendant to use in the subsequent steps of the operation.

With this grapple effected, the defendant raises or lowers the grappled arm to protect himself from a possible blow from the assailant's left fist, the latter raising his arm with the intention of striking the defendant about the head and face.

At this point, the defendant strides forward on his left foot, draws the assailant's grappled arm under his extended left arm and thrusts his "haunches" close against the assailant's right side (Illustration No. 64). The defendant's extended arm wards off the blow from the assailant's raised left arm (Illustration No. 64) and when that is accomplished the arm is hooked around the assailant's entrapped arm, holding in it an "arm-breaking" position (Illustration No 65) constituting a most effective "submission."

Rubbing your radial bone, in a slight up and down motion, against Triple Warmer 11 can have great results. There needs to be a "two way action"

TW 11

within this technique. The opponent's hand needs to be pushed down while pressure is applied upwards on the Triple Warmer point.

The technique described in Illustration No. 63 uses your neck to break the opponent's arm. Once you have achieved the desired position, you must point the opponent's palm upward, since Triple Warmer 11 needs an angle, perpendicular to the point to injure the arm.

The author alludes to an "arm-breaking" position in Ilustration No. 65. It is not quite that simple. To increase the effectiveness of this technique, I would suggest grappling your gi, shirt, jacket, etc. after you have hooked your arm around the opponent's arm. The clothing will give you more leverage as you apply the lock.

LESSON NINETEEN

IRI-TORI-UMAKUI-ATE — "SCARF-HOLDING-FOR-A-VITAL-TOUCH."

The familiar grapple by which the contestant seizes his opponent's scarfs is the one chosen to the initiate the operation of "scarf-holding for a vital touch."

It is assumed that the assailant grasps the defendant's scarfs with both his hands (Illustration No. 66) and that the defendant effects no grapple whatever.

IL. 66

IL. 67

Grasping the defendant firmly in this position the assailant gives a sudden pull to the defendant and proceeds at once to apply the "touch." To do this, he brings the top of his head in violent contact with the defendant's upper jaw (U, Fig. 2, Chart) at the center of the upper lip (Illustration No. 67).

Although there is a certain point at which the assailant's head must touch the defendant's jaw, the upper lip each side of the median line and nose will suffer more or less from the impact of the assailant's head.

The force required for the "touch" varies according to the rigidity with which the defendant holds his head. The assailant first lowers his head and then raises it so as to bring the center of the top of his head against the defendant's upper jaw.

The effect of the "touch" will be different according to the force with which it is given and the constitution of the one who suffers it. It is usually dealt so that it produces unconsciousness for a few moments, but it is capable of inducing more serious results, which can only be counteracted by the prompt appliance of Katsu or "vivification." If the contestant delivering the "touch" should be so disposed he could inflict serious injury upon his opponent by means of this "touch."

The sensation experienced by the recipient of the "touch" is one of intense pain. It is a matter of conjecture whether the pain produces unconsciousness or whether it arises from the shock and jar to the brain.

The fact, however, that a blow on the jaw sufficient to break the teeth does not necessarily render the victim unconscious, seems to prove that it is not the pain that is the immediate cause of the unconscious state.

The precise moment at which this "vital-touch" is to be given is, according to the ancient Jiu-Jitsuan text, at "the ebbing and rising of the vital tide," or in other words, at a certain point in the respiration when the breath is expelled.

The exact moment can only be determined by watching the breathing of the assailant and then making the attack when his lungs are deflated.

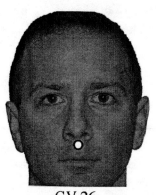

GV 26

Governor Vessel 26 ("Middle of Person") lies at the base of the nose on upper third of the Philtrum. It is known to calm the mind, clear the senses, and promote resuscitation. These attributes tell us that it can cause the opposite reaction in your opponent should you use this very potent point. While the author uses the forehead to attack this point, it is easier to attack using the knuckles of either hand in a rubbing motion. The opponent will find intense pain, as well as vision impairment when this point is rubbed vigorously.

We now revisit the extraordinary point known as M-HN 18. This point is ideal for the technique demonstrated in Illustration 67. There are a few caveats, however. If you opponenent is the same size as you, then it would be natural to throw your head onto one of these points. If you opponent is taller than you, then it would be difficult to perform the technique in this manner. You then have a few choices providing that your head is to be used as a hammer. The first one being to knuckle into GV 26 as described above and the second one is to use the top of your head and strike Stomach 5 in and up towards the ear.

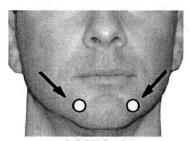

M-HN 18

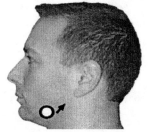

ST 5

LESSON TWENTY

SUIGETSU-ATE — "VITAL-TOUCH-AT-STOMACH."

The contest of Suigetsu is inaugurated by the assailant as he seizes the defendant's wrist (Illustration No. 68).

The defendant, as his wrists are seized and drawn forward, raises his left foot and placing his left knee upon the forearm of the assailant's right arm (Illustration No. 69), forces it down thus wrenching off the assailant's hold on his left wrist. When this has been accomplished, the defendant raises his right foot and wrenches free from the assailant's grapple on his right wrist in the same manner that he employed in releasing his left wrist. This is accomplished more by the pain inflicted than by the force required to bend the assailant's arm when the pressure of the knee is enforced.

IL. 68

The left hand of the defendant, which is freed from the assailant's grapple, grasps the right arm of the assailant while the latter's grapple with his left hand is being released.

When the right arm is free, the defendant bends it at the elbow, and, striding forward on his right foot, thrusts the point of the crooked elbow (S. Fig. 2 Chart) against the assailant's stomach (Illustration No. 70). No swinging of the arm is required but the elbow should be applied with considerable force.

The assailant immediately suffers intense pain and if the blow has been given with sufficient force, he may lose consciousness.

When the victim of the "touch" does not regain consciousness in a few seconds, a Katsu or "vivification" method will be found necessary.

IL. 69

That a "vital touch" may be very effectively delivered at the stomach is evident from the fact that one of the greatest nerve centers of the body is located there, rendering that part of the body particularly susceptible to the successful operation of the Jiu-Jitsuan.

It is a very simple matter to produce instant death by the "stomach touch" — not even the wonderful Katsu methods possessing the power to restore the one thus affected

IL. 70

58

There are a few different points that we are going to discuss in further detail as we go through this lesson. Our discussion will focus on body points.

Front view of torso

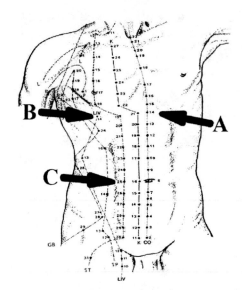

Vital Torso Points

A points to Conception Vessel 14. This point is known as "Great Palace." It sits slightly below the Zyphoid Process on the midline of the body. Pain in the cardiac region, and chest, and palpitations are some of the disorders that this point is used to treat. This again tells us that with proper force and intent, an opponent can be injured when struck on this point, straight in as if we were to penetrate the body.

B refers to Liver 14, which has been previously discussed in earlier lessons.

C is an interesting point. Stomach 25 is the warning point for the Large Intestine meridian. This point lies on either side of the navel approximately 2 inches. When struck in and down with a 1 knuckle fist, it can cause the hips to give out and the opponent to fall. On a more severe strike, it can render the opponent unconscious. As he falls he will be unable to protect himself from the floor. Use this point with caution.

Other options to go along with these points, incase the opponent's balance gets disrupted and his body shifts to one side or the other are: Spleen 17 ("Food's Cavity") and Spleen 21 ("big Wrapping") are excellent points to strike should the opponent's body turn to the left or right. Both points will effect the opponent's breathing making it difficult for him to continue his aggression. Conception Vessel 14 ("Great Palace"), as shown in Illustration No. 70 is a great point to strike if the opponent's body stays square. It is know to clear the heart and calm the mind, thus telling us that we can adversely affect the body when struck with intent.

ATE-NO-KOKOROE—"METHODS-OF-DEALING-VITAL TOUCH-ES."
Akenoma—"Thumb-on-the-Throat."

Preparatory to administering the Akenoma "touch," the assailant effects a grapple with each hand on the scarfs of the defendant (Illustration No. 71).

Holding the defendant in this position, the assailant gives a sudden pull to his opponent's body and extends the thumb of his right hand, the scarf being firmly held between the palm and fingers, the release of the thumb

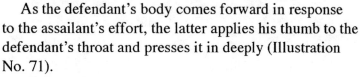

IL. 71

having no effect on the stability of the grapple.

As the defendant's body comes forward in response to the assailant's effort, the latter applies his thumb to the defendant's throat and presses it in deeply (Illustration No. 71).

The point of contact at which this pressure is exerted is in the little hollow between the points of the sternum or breast-bone. This is where the windpipe is most exposed and consequently it can be more easily compressed at the point than any other.

The result of this "vital-touch" will, of course, depend upon the length of time the pressure is exerted and the force with which the thumb is applied.

If the stoppage of the breath be prolonged so as to produce strangulation, a "vivification" method will be required to restore the victim of the "touch."

The effects of the Akenoma "touch" are exactly the same as those obtained by a "neck-wringing" process, but they are secured with much greater ease by means of Akenoma than by any other Jiu-Jistuian method.

The Akenoma "touch" is one of the most effective methods know in Jiu-Jitsu of defending oneself against several assailants. It can be so quickly applied and with such absolute certainty as to enable a person suddenly attacked to dispose of several enemies with very little exertion and in an incredibly short time.

This is an interesting technique as there are many more options than were originally shown. While it is true that a strike to the wind pipe can either temporarily or permanently incapacitate your opponent, modern times and modern laws dictate a different approach to non-military personal. After all, we have to remember that this book was originally written to catalog the lessons that were taught to the Japanese Military.

Vital points of the neck

For purposes of our discussion, we are going to focus on temporarily incapcitating our oponent. Point A sits on Conception Vessel 22 ("Heavenly Projection"). This point can be utilized without disrupting the wind pipe. When you press in and down, and then slightly to the heart side, the opponent will get a heavy feeling in his chest as he attempts to turn his left side away for you. this is ideal, especially if he has grapped your lapels with both hands.

Point B refers to Stomach 9 which has been covered in Lesson 13. The pressure is applied with your thumb and you are to drive your thumb in and down if the opponent is your height or shorter, and in and up if they are taller.

You must always take into consideration the size of your opponent relative to your size when choosing which technique to use and which point to "accessorize" your technique.

LESSON TWENTY-TWO

ATE-NO-KOKOROE—
"METHODS-OF-DEALING-VITAL TOUCHES."
Komekami—"Lower-Jaw."

More "vital touches" can be effected on the front of the body than on the back and for this reason each contestant should be careful to avoid facing his opponent directly, as they approach each other, until the danger of receiving a "vital touch" is lessened by the engagement of the hands and arms.

IL. 72

When the Komekami "touch" is to be applied, the assailant should allow his opponent to approach at the side and back. It is here assumed that the defendant comes up behind the assailant and is allowed to seize the latter's left arm (Illustration no. 72).

This grapple engages one arm of each contestant, but does not secure either one from the possibility of a "touch" by means of the free arm.

IL. 73

When the combatants face each other (Illustration No. 73), each one grasping an arm of the other, the "lower jaw touch" is possible to either. It is here assumed that the assailant delivers the "touch" with the point of his elbow (Illustration No. 74), though it can be given with the fist just as well, if the grapple is such as to place the contestants further away from each other than is indicated here.

The point at which the "lower jaw touch" is to be delivered is just blow the ear on the curve of the jaw (Ko, Fig. 2, Chart). The force with which the blow is delivered is acquired by swinging the arm. The nearer to the ear that the blow is administered the more intense will be the pain and the greater the shock.

The jar to the brain that is the result of this "touch" will produce dizziness and if sufficient force be exerted, unconsciousness.

The contestant who delivers a "vital touch" should always be prepared to deliver a second "touch" at another point in case the first "touch" fails in its purpose. This "re-touch" does not mean the repetition of the first "touch" but the administration of a "vital touch" at another spot.

If one hand or arm be used in delivering a "touch," the other arm should be in readiness for the "re-touch," so that if one fails, the other arm will be in

62

position to deliver a second "touch." But if one arm is engaged in a grapple, thus leaving but one arm free, this free arm will have to be employed in delivering both the "touch" and the "re-touch."

The "re-touch" in this instance to be delivered is the Umakui or "upper jaw touch." This blow may be delivered with the hand (Illustration No. 75). In a previous lesson, it was given with the top of the head.

The heel of the palm is the part of the hand that is used in the "re-touch." It should be hardened by constant practice in hitting a hard surface in order to be effective in the "touch."

IL. 74

IL. 75

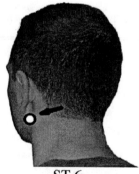
ST 6

Stomach 6, when used in the manner described in this lesson, can cause unconsciousness and dislocation of the jaw. Notice the angle in Illustration 74 and the picture to the left. The angle that is demonstrated in Illustration 74 is a back to front strike with the elbow. This not only follows the jaw line, follows the path of the facial nerve. Understanding basic anatomy is essential to understanding the deeper aspects of all martial arts.

Point A sits on what is known as the 3rd eye. The location is dead center between the eyebrows. Struck in and up can cause dizziness and lead to unconsciousness depending on the force and intent of the strike.

Point B sits where the protuberance of the nose joins the skull and needs to be struck in a downward manner. This may not break the nose, but it can cause dizziness and watering of the eyes,.

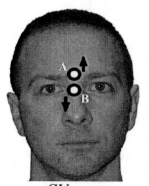
GV

ATE-NO-KOKOROE—
"METHODS-OF-DEALING-VITAL TOUCHES."
Atama—"Counter-touch-at-Base-of-Brain."

Attention has previously been called to the fact that in dealing a "vital touch" one should be prepared to deliver a "re-touch" in case the first "touch" should fail to produce the desired effect. There is nothing more dangerous to a contestant than to fail in an effort, because the advantage is thereby given to the opponent and his own exertion may be used in his defeat.

The failure of a "touch" when unsupported by a "re-touch" leads to a

IL. 76

IL. 77

IL. 78

"counter-touch."

In this instance, the assailant who has attempted to deliver a "stomach touch" with his left fist is foiled by the defendant who proceeds at once to effect a "counter-touch." As the assailant makes the thrust with his left arm, the defendant parries it with his left arm (Illustration No. 76). The force with which the blow is delivered tends to swing the defendant around, bringing his right side against the left side of the assailant (Illustration No. 77).

In this position, the assailant's back is fully exposed to the attack of the defendant as the latter draws nearer with the intention of administering a "vital touch" (Illustration No. 78).

The point selected upon which the "touch" is to be applied is at the base of the brain (V. t, Fig 1, Chart). The blow is delivered with the knuckles of the right fist. The usual results of a "touch," dizziness and unconsciousness follow.

The "touch" is practically painless when delivered by a proficient Jiu-Jitsuian. While it is an efficient mode of disabling an assailant in actual combat, it is equally effective in a formal contest where it is desir-

A strike to the back of the head can unquestionably cause unconsciousness or even death. There have been deaths that have occurred when someone has fallen and hit their head on the floor or an object on the way down.

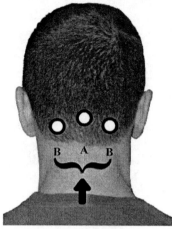

There are two vital points that will be discussed in relation to this lesson. There are many methods with which to strike these points.

Point **A** is Governor Vessel 16 also known as "Wind Palace." This point is known to clear the mind and nourish the brain. It is also a great point to stop nose bleeds. GV 16 lies in the hollow space, where the cervical spine joins the skull. The angle and direction is up and in towards the forehead.

In Illustration No. 78, the strike that is demonstrated is an elbow strike. This is but one of many strikes that can be dealt at this point.

Depending on how you get behind the opponent determines your striking surface. If you are in close proximity, as in Illustration No. 78, the the elbow will work well. Half a step back, though, you will have to use a palm strike or an upper cut. If you are in front of the opponent, who is grabbing your lapels and pulling you forward, you can employ a back to front strike towards the forehead. Your opponent's reaction will not be to lurch foreward, but he will go up on his toes and back.

Point B is Gallbladder 20 which has been discussed in a previous lesson. Again, your striking surface depends on your proximity to your opponent.

LESSON TWENTY-FOUR

IRI-TORI-UMAKUI—"SCARF-HOLDING-FOR-VITAL-TOUCH."
Ura-Ate—"Defense-by-Vital Touch."

When an attempt to administer the Umakui "touch" has been frustrated by the employment of an "arm-breaking" process, the attack may be renewed by the administration of another "vital touch", Ro (R, Fig.2, Chart).

The grapples required for dealing this "touch" are the same as those assumed in delivering the Umakui "touch," with the exception that the Umakui grapple is taken so as to prevent the free movement of the defendant's head, whereas, in dealing the Ro "touch" there is not such restriction.

IL. 79

When the holds are assumed by the assailant on the defendant's scarfs, the assailant then raises his right knee and brings it up with great force between the defendant's legs, (Illustration No. 79) striking the testicles. This is followed by intense pain and unconsciousness is usually the result; and it can be given with such force as to produce death. The "stomach touch" and Ro are the most dangerous ones to be used in Jiu-Jitsu and should only be used as a mode of self-preservation when violently attacked.

In the case of each of these "touches," the pressure of a great nerve-center is what renders the "touch" so effective and so painful.

The inside of the leg has points that are extremely vulnerable to attack. Not much force is required to drop even a much larger opponent. In the lesson above, the strike is focused towards the groin. While this is a great place to strike, there are certain things that have to be taken into account. If you are very close to the opponent while executing this strike, his reaction will be that of bending forward very quickly. Your head is wide open for him to unwittingly strike your head with his. This has been covered in a previous lesson, but you were the one executing the technique, not the opponent.

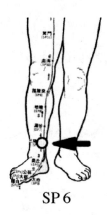

SP 6

The first point that can be used with an instep kick is Spleen 6. This point is known as the "Triple Yin Crossing" due to the fact that three meridians cross at this point located approximately 3 fingers up from the ankle bone. A kick in and down on this point will release the ankle, and then the knee and hip. At that point you can follow up to the opponent's groin or other points that we will now discuss.

Liver 9 ("Yin Wrapping") is another initiatory point before going to the groin, or it can be a finishing point after kicking Spleen 6. With enough force, a strike to Liver 9 can release the knee and drop your opponent.

The last set of points that we are going to discuss with relation to this lesson is the inguinal crease. Located in the crease on either side of the genitals, a strike to this area can severely injure and even kill an opponent.

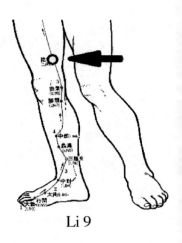

Li 9

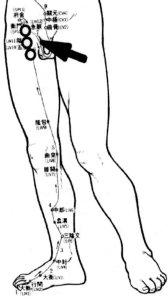

Inguinal Crease

The points associated with this area are Liver 10 ("Five Measures on the Foot"), 11 ("Yin Modesty"), and 12 ("Urgent Channel") and sit on top of the Femoral nerve. Struck straight in with a knee or even a punch, these points, either combined with previous points in this book or on their own, can free you from many situations.

All of these points are fantastic for close quarter grappling.

LESSON TWENTY-FIVE

KATSU — "VIVIFICATION."

When the victim of a "vital touch" does not regain consciousness in a short time and the heart action and breathing reach such a low point that death may perhaps ensue, it is time to resort to Katsu or "vivification."

All " vital touches" are not capable of producing a dangerous state of unconsciousness, but two of the "vital touches" — the "stomach touch" and Ro "touch," when administered by a skilled Jiu-Jitsuian may easily result in a condition that would terminate in death were it not for the application of Katsu.

When the one who is to administer "vivification" has examined the victim and ascertained that life is not extinct, the victim should be disrobed if his clothing be tight and if it is not, it should be loosened so as to facilitate his breathing.

IL. 80

The assailant then stoops and raises the defendant to a sitting posture (Illustration No. 80), passing his left arm around the chest and pressing it, at the same time, gently hitting the defendant's back with the palm of his hand. The region at which the pain is applied is over the spine at the seventh rib, the blows thus stimulating the pneumogastric nerves (K, Fig. 1, Chart).

The pressure on the chest and the blows with the palm on the back should be given as the victim is exhaling. This aids in the contraction and the inflation of the lungs and the stimulation of the nerves that control the action of the heart.

As the victim begins to revive, his name should be called loudly in his ears. This stimulates the auditory nerves and adds to the general excitation of the nervous system, which must be accomplished before the "vivification" is complete.

This process is called Raiko, meaning literally, "lightening," probably from the fact that when it is administered by a skilled Jiu-Jitsuian it is done with such lightning-like rapidity as to render the "secrets" of the method imperceptible to the observer.

While Raiko is a form of "vivification" that is effective in most forms of suspended animation, or unconsciousness, there is another one designed to follow it when the condition of a victim is so serious as to require more effective means of restoration than is afforded by Raiko.

In administering Kensei, which means "restoring the dead,"—the assailant stands behind the defendant and applies his hands on the shoulders. The thumbs are pressed deeply into the shoulder near the neck, where the thinness of the muscles and other tissues leaves the nerves grouped at this point most exposed. This vital spot is just at the pectoral arch, where the scapula and clavicle meet. The fingers of each hand extend over the shoulder in front (Illustration No. 81).

IL. 81

If the victim is not wholly unconscious, the pressure of the thumbs will cause intense pain, and if he be unconscious, the pain and consequent stimulation of the nerves controlling the action of the heart and lungs will revive him.

The "vivification" method for the treatment of Ro is especially adapted to the "touch." It consists of a kick with the toes of the foot on the victim's back over the third from the last vertebrae and is delivered while the assailant is administering the Kensei "touch"

As you will notice, much of this book deals with taking an opponent out. A critical component, in life itself, is the ability to heal. Though there is only one lesson here, I will attempt to further describe this basic method of revival included in this lesson.

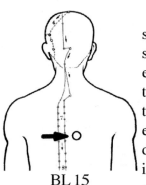

BL 15

Using Illustration No. 80 as an example, you are to sit your partner up. The area on the back that is to be struck is Bladder 15 or the Heart "Shu" point. Located near the 7th Thoracic Vertebrae, this point is used to assist in revival. In terms of the use for this lesson, the opponent is unconsious and we need to "influence" the heart with a strike on his right side in the direction of the right arm. The reason for the strike in this manner is that the nerves coming off the right side of the spine flows in that direction. Striking this way sends the message along the nerve pathway, thus "stimulating the heart.

69

When I say "strike", this implies to hit with enough force, gently, to send the signal along the nerve path. Too strong a strike becomes simply blunt trauma and the body will over ride this stimuli. Injury can also occur from blunt force trauma and we do not want to put the patient into more jeopardy than they are already in.

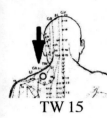

TW 15

Triple Warmer 15, or "Heavenly Crevice," is located on the back, center of the Trapezius muscle in a hollow crevice, hence its name. Using your thumbs, as described above in a manner like you are trying to penetrate through the pectoral muscle (down and forward on the point), you will get maximum effect, according to the lesson.

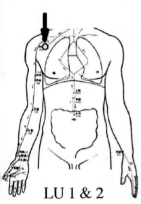

LU 1 & 2

The other point that is used in conjunction with Triple Warmer 15 is Lung 1 & 2. Lung 1 is known as "Central Residence," and Lung 2 as "Cloud Gate." Pressing down and then pulling back on the shoulders activates both points and stimulates the lungs. The pushing and pulling effort also forces the diaphragm to expand and contract to assist the victim in breathing. Simultaneously, your right knee is in the person's back, not directly on the spine, but against the Bladder 13, 14, 15 points. This also stimulates the heart related nerves as they come off the spine. As you pull the shoulders back and stimulate the Lung points, you are to bend your right knee and apply pressure into the above points

Appendix A:
Chart 1 - Rear View of the Body

V.t -   Governor Vessel 16

V.t (T) -   Gall Bladder 20

K -   Bladder 15

I -   Gall Bladder 25

Sg -   Bladder 23

K(R) -   Governor Vessel 2

    This list was compiled using Qpuncture 2. It is an interactive resource. For more information please log onto www.LearnPressurePoints.com.

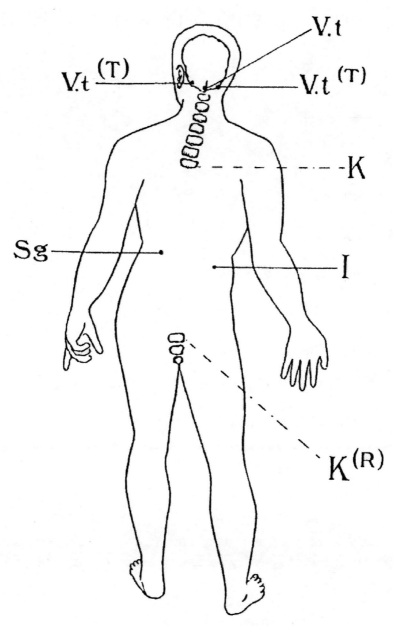

Fig. 1. The Chart

Apendix A

Appendix B:
Chart 2 - Front View of the Body

U - Governor Vessel 26 (Lesson 19)

Ko - Stomach 6 (Lesson 22)

Ka - Stomach 12

Kb - Stomach 12

Ma - Stomach 5 (Lesson 5)

Mb - Stomach 5 (Lesson 5)

A - Stomach 9 / Conception Vessel 22 (Lesson 21)

S - Conception Vessel 14 (Lesson 20)

T - Pericardium 6 (Lesson 20)

R - The testicles and/or the inguinal crease. (Lesson 24)

This list was compiled using Qpuncture 2. It is an interactive resource. For more information please log onto www.LearnPressurePoints.com.

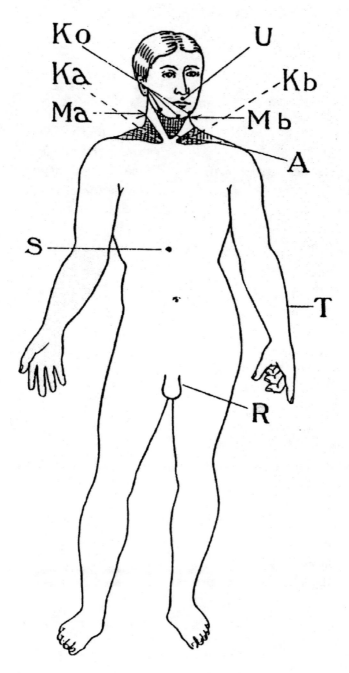

Fig. 2. The Chart

Apendix B

Selected Bibliography & Sources

Dillman, George
Kyusho Jitsu
Dillman Karate International
Reading, PA 1992

Dillman, George
Ryukyu Kempo
Dillman Karate International
Reading, PA 1992

Dillman, George
Tuite
Dillman Karate International
Reading, PA 1992

Ellis, Andrew, et. al.
Grasping the Wind
Paradigm Publications
Brookline, MA 1988

Qpuncture, Inc.
QPuncture 1 &2
Qpuncture Inc.
Los Angeles, CA 2001

Jay, Wally
Small Circle Jujitsu
Ohara Publications
Burbank, CA 1989

Wilson-Pauwels, Akeson, Stewart
**Cranial Nerves: Anatomy and
Clinical Comments**
B.C Decker, Inc.
Philadelphia, 1988